I0041659

AGILE TEAM FACILITATOR

MARTIN ALAIMO

AGILE TEAM FACILITATOR

CHIEF AGILITY OFFICER SERIES
A Coach's Path Towards Enterprise Agility

kleer

2016

Copyright © 2016 Martin Alaimo

ISBN: 978-0-9975796-2-8

All rights reserved. No part of this book may be used, reproduced, stored in or introduced into a retrieval system or transmitted in any form or by any means (electronic, mechanical, photocopying, recording, or otherwise) without the written permission of the publisher, except in the case of brief quotations in critical reviews and certain other noncommercial uses permitted by copyright law.

First edition: June 2016

Copyediting: Alejandra Bello - www.mundo-bello.com

Cover and editorial design: Martin Alaimo

Interior illustrations: Martin Alaimo

Published by:

Shive One LLC
16192 Coastal Highway
Lewes, Delaware 19958 USA

This book is published in a variety of formats. Some of the material included with the printed version of this book may not be included in electronic versions.

It often happens. You open a book and find out that the author has dedicated it to someone else. I don't want this to be the case.

I want to invite you to follow a path together. To talk, exchange ideas, think possibilities and manage to create a better world of work, together.

This book is dedicated to your inner facilitator. If he is already there, so be it! If not, let's discover it.

CONTENTS

INTRODUCTION

~~CHIEF~~ AGILITY OFFICER(S)?

> *That the Dilbert cartoons have become cultural icons says much about the extent to which organizations can make work miserable and pointless. (Laloux, 2014)*

For a number of years and each time more intensely, I feel that life in traditional organizations is coming to an end. It doesn't matter who I speak with, from the newest employee to the highest ranking manager and even the biggest client, I perceive more disillusionment than enthusiasm. Given this scenario, it is not strange that a movement such as Agility has found fertile ground for its growth.

I also come across organizations willing to adopt an agile model, as if it was only a question of simply connecting a pen drive, without taking into consideration the cultural changes necessary to be able to transform the historical paradigms of an organization in this new way of understanding the working and business world.

In these cases, we still need to understand that an exciting, inspiring, innovative and disruptive work context is not reached by imitating the proposals of Agility in traditional organizations. Before doing so, I think it is necessary to consider two key issues to cultivate the agile paradigm:

- The obsolescence of the chief figure as we know it.
- The need to develop an agile and servant leadership.

CHIEF: NO MORE CHIEFS

> *"**Chief:** A leader or ruler of a people or clan".*
>
> *Oxford Dictionary of English*

It may sound strong, it may sound radical and even pretentious; it is something I have discovered along these almost 14 years of contact with enterprise agility and that I consider one of the most fundamental of all the aspects I intend to cover in this series of books: if we don't assume that the role of chief is functional to more traditional paradigms and that in an agile ecosystem it becomes obsolete, sooner or later, we will be asking ourselves why our organization does not get the typical benefits of this new way of seeing the world of work.

In an agile culture, people are no longer at the service of a chief who tells them what to do and how to do it, that gives them a space of opinion but without the possibility of vote. In Agility, people find themselves supported by a servant-leader who generates contexts where each of the teams find their optimal point of self-organization, growth and awareness of their work environment.

Agility Officer(s): Agile Leaders

I am convinced that the second most important factor in an agile culture is the behavior of the leaders of the organization.

The most powerful mechanisms of communicating their beliefs, convictions and intentions is that which they systematically pay attention to (Schein, 2010). If an organization intends to be agile, it needs all its leaders to think and act in an agile way. Either in meetings, their treatment to suppliers, in the kind of recognition to others, in the way they plan, etc. Otherwise, they will be transmitting a contradictory message.

In fact, the **primary mechanisms** through which the culture of an organization is determined are related to the behavior of its leaders (Schein, 2010), for instance:

- What they pay attention to, measure and control on a regular basis.
- Their reaction to critical incidents and organizational crisis.
- How they allocate resources.
- The teaching and coaching they provide.
- The design of rewards and *status.*
- The way in which they recruit, select, promote and exclude people.

Other mechanisms work as **secondary or back up factors**, such as:

- Organizational design and structure.
- Organizational systems and procedures.
- Organizational rites and rituals.
- Design of physical space: facades and buildings.
- Stories about events and important people.

- Formal statements of organizational philosophy, creed (vision, mission, values) and constitution or regulations.

THE CULTURE OF AN ORGANIZATION IS DETERMINED BY THE BEHAVIOR OF ITS LEADERS.

Agile Coaching: A Profession

Profound changes are taking place in the corporate world, not only in the way of doing business but also in the way companies are structured, teams are lead, and work is managed.

In tune with these changes a fundamental role has consolidated: the **agile coach**, as a facilitator, catalyzer and change agent. This new role has given origin to an emerging profession.

In the last years, agile coaching as a discipline has become more and more relevant and more and more professionals have become involved in it. Referents, theories, and various proposals have emerged, which manage different aspects and performance areas.

These are some of the people who have inspired me through their work, our collaboration, our conversations or exchange of ideas. To name just a few of them: Mike Cohn, Lyssa Adkins, Tobias Mayer, Olaf Lewitz, Juan Gabardini, Pablo Tortorella, Pete Behrens, Hiroshi Hiromoto, Roger Brown, Diana Larsen, Esther Derby; as well as many others who also contributed significantly to this movement.

Whenever I get involved as an agile coach in an organization, I see wonderful things happening. Not only regarding the organization itself but also regarding myself as a person. I can honestly say that I love this profession and greatly enjoy doing what I do. However, it is not always a bed of roses. Throughout the years, I could observe three things that have called my attention:

- Often, the people who are taking their first steps in the agility world ask me about which, in my opinion, are the steps to follow when it comes to becoming a professional coach.

15

- Also, and with similar frequency, I find agile coaching professionals with whom I don't share a common universe of concepts, abilities, tools and opinions when discussing cases, situations or, what to me is the most important, when providing agile coaching in an organization.
- In the past years, only 40% of the candidates managed to obtain the certification *Certified Enterprise Coaches* (*CECs*) of the *Scrum Alliance*[1] (Behrens, 2011).

I think the reason that is common to these three issues is that many professionals involved in the agile environment are still lacking a deeper understanding of the responsibilities, the abilities, and training necessary for a person to become a coach. Nowadays, I have the impression that each new agile coach that is born does it with his own conception of the profession. Therefore, there are agile trainers, consultants, mentors, facilitators, appraisers, project managers, all roles with substantial differences in the way they do things, although they are all self-called *agile coaches.*

Due to all this diversity, I set out to trace a possible route for enterprise agility professionals to be able to incorporate the knowledge and abilities that the exercise of this beautiful profession requires.

AGILE COACHING: A PROPOSAL

Next, I'll share with you a proposal about what agile coaching could and could not be. In order to do that, I assume it is an

---

[1] http://www.scrumalliance.org

extension of professional coaching according to the definition by the *International Coach Federation* (ICF)[2].

The ICF defines coaching as the as partnering with clients in a thought-provoking and creative process, that inspires them to maximize their personal and professional potential, which is particularly important in today's uncertain and complex environment. Coaches honor the client as the expert in his or her life and work and believe every client is creative, resourceful and whole. Standing on this foundation, the coach's responsibility is to:

- Discover, clarify, and align with what the client wants to achieve.
- Encourage client self-discovery
- Elicit client-generated solutions and strategies
- Hold the client responsible and accountable

This process helps clients dramatically improve their outlook on work and life, while improving their leadership skills and unlocking their potential.

At the same time, I support Adkins vision, which considers agile coaching as a group of similar disciplines: facilitation, mentoring, coaching and training (Adkins, 2010).

AGILE COACHING IS NOT ONLY ABOUT KNOWLEDGE TRANSFER

In a teacher-student relationship, the first one is the one who has the knowledge of a certain subject, while the second one is the one interested in acquiring that knowledge. A relationship thus formulated implies a knowledge transfer from one person to another or to others.

---

[2] http://www.coachfederation.org/

Many times (luckily less and less)[3], there is a clear difference in hierarchy between the teacher, who considers himself superior, and the learner who has an inferiority position in the relationship. The learner adopts, in many cases, a passive position, anxious, in his relationship with the person who is teaching, who has more of an active role.

The raw material of this kind of teaching is knowledge: what the teacher knows and the learner doesn't.

Unlike this traditional way of teaching, in professional coaching, there aren't hierarchical differences. The coach and his client are both equal.

IN AGILE COACHING, THE CLIENT AND THE COACH ARE EQUAL.

AGILE COACHING IS NOT ONLY CONSULTING

The relationship that exists between a consultant and his client is mainly based on the solutions that the consultant can provide to solve the client's problems or needs.

The consultant is usually an expert and has a lot of knowledge in a particular area. It can be considered that the relationship is established based on the solutions that the consultant is able to provide and that, many times, is in charge of implementing.

---

[3] There isn't necessarily a relationship of hierarchy in all cases (it happens in round classrooms which include students and teachers and the democratizing word of the retrospective)

Unlike this kind of consultancy, coaching does not intend to provide solutions to the client's problems, but to help the client observe his context from new perspectives which would allow him to find his own, more genuine solutions.

AGILE COACHING HELPS THE CLIENT OBSERVE HIS CONTEXT FROM NEW PERSPECTIVES.

AGILE COACHING IS NOT ONLY MENTORING

The relationship between the mentor and the mentee is a relationship based on the experience that the first has in a specific subject that he can use to guide and support the second, so the mentee develops the desired abilities by practicing them. The element that allows for the existence of this relationship is the experience that the mentor has and transmits.

Unlike mentoring, coaching does not intend to set an example from experience, but to constantly defy the client's creed, perspectives, and common sense.

AGILE COACHING DEFIES THE CLIENT'S BELIEFS

Agile coaching is not only facilitation

Facilitation covers all the activities and tasks that the facilitator performs, to allow a certain group of people to have a meaningful conversation with a common purpose [take decisions, solve problems, exchange ideas and information].

The facilitator helps the group focus collective conversations. He does not lead the group or tries to distract or entertain. This relationship is based on the dynamic that the facilitator creates with the group of people.

Unlike facilitation, coaching does not intend to help a working group carry out an effective and collaborative meeting, but it is focused on individuals and teams who are centered on self-discovery and achieving an apprenticeship that broadens their possibilities.

Agile coaching is focused on people and teams who want to learn and broaden their possibilities.

A Coach's Path Towards Enterprise Agility

My proposal is to consider this profession an extension of professional coaching and a path that consists of many different steps.

To trace this path I consider an agile coach can take, I am basing on the road map proposed by the International Consortium for

Agility (ICAgile)[4]; and complement this approach with some personal views.

Below, I'll show you the road that I propose and invite you to take.

1. Scrum Master

The majority of the professionals, who take their first steps in the agility world as a work model, do it through a framework known as *Scrum*. The *Scrum Master* is the one who helps the teams use *Scrum* in a meaningful way. I like to call this stage "station zero", to highlight the idea that this is just the beginning of the road for an agile coach. The profession goes much further than the knowledge and meaningful use of *Scrum*.

To be a scrum master is only the beginning of the road for an agile coach.

---

2. Agile team facilitator

There are also many professionals who enter agility through other methodologies, tools or frameworks. We cannot call them *Scrum Masters* since they are not linked to *Scrum*. In any case, the facilitator of agile teams has developed the facilitation

---

[4]https://www.icagile.com/files/2014.AgileCoaching.pdf

skills required for supporting the team in participative decision-making, conflict resolution, and self-organization. If this professional has evolved from station zero, then he performs as Scrum Master and has also developed these skills, which are now part of his/her toolbox.

The facilitator works with one or two agile teams where he facilitates activities and is not responsible or is not yet qualified to carry out agile transformation initiatives.

THE FACILITATOR OF AGILE TEAMS WORKS WITH ONE OR TWO TEAMS.

---

3. AGILE COACH

An agile coach is a facilitator of agile teams who has reached the expert level in Agility. He or she has developed more advanced skills in facilitation, training and mentoring, and at the same time can clearly differentiate between these disciplines.

Additionally, to his or her facilitation, mentoring and leadership skills, he or she has incorporated professional coaching skills. His or her focus elevates to a multiple teams' level and is supported by this family of disciplines.

An agile coach provides coaching and/or mentoring to Scrum Masters and agile team facilitators. The focus of the agile coach is in the relationship that exists between the different teams from the same department or area within the organization and has developed enough experience to initiate the transformation of the teams towards agility.

This level is a possible landing point for many agile coaches (Adkins, 2010). In the words of the *Agile Coaching Institute*, "if we had more qualified agile coaches, Agility would be much healthier"[5].

THE FOCUS OF THE AGILE COACH IS ON THE RELATIONSHIP THAT EXISTS BETWEEN THE DIFFERENT TEAMS.

4. ENTERPRISE AGILE COACH

At this level, the agile coach has incorporated systemic abilities: he can listen to the conversation at an organizational level, doing executive coaching to the enterprise leadership team, and identify the different organizational cultures. He knows about cultural change management and is able to facilitate strategies to overcome organizational resistance.

An enterprise agile coach works with more operational levels as well as strategic, Scrum Masters, facilitators, managers, executives and c-Levels.

---

[5]http://www.agilecoachinginstitute.com/coaching-courses-industry-certifications/

AN ENTERPRISE AGILE COACH IS ABLE TO WORK AT ANY LEVEL OF THE ORGANIZATION.

EVIDENCE GENERATION

At any of these levels, the professional generates continuous evidence for the community (colleagues and organizations) which makes him enough of an expert to approach a certain level. Although it is a significant contribution, attending courses and/or workshops is not enough to reach an expert level. In order to do that, it will be necessary for him to experiment, to do and share.

MY PURPOSE, A CONFESSION.

Thanks to a series of conversations, I had during Agile 2014 in Orlando, with Gustavo Quiroz, Roger Brown, Lyssa Adkins, Luis Mulato, Hiroshi Hiromoto, Michael Sahota, Dhaval Panchal, Pete Behrens and Claudia Sandoval I think I discovered a new dimension in my purpose regarding Agility. I still believe we need organizations that are more humane, happier workers, and contexts of more innovation. I also believe we need to raise the expectation bar we have of agile coaches. Therefore, from now on, I set myself in getting actively involved in contributing to transform agile coaching into a profession in itself, to get more and better agile coaches.

It is in this sense that I have decided to kick off this series of publications which will deal with the different aspects of the agile coach's profession.

This book focusing on the facilitator of agile teams is the first book of a series that will deal with the following subjects:

- Book 2: Agile Team Coach
- Book 3: Agile Trainer
- Book 4: Enterprise Agility Coach
- Book 5: Agile Executive Coach

I invite you to visit the ~~Chief~~ Agility Officer(s)[6] website and subscribe to the news list to find out about the future publication dates.

---

[6] http://chiefagilityofficer.com

CONTENTS OF BOOK 1

This first book focuses on the agile team facilitator role, which is seen as the first step towards developing into an enterprise agile coach.

Chapter 2 is dedicated to showing the discipline of facilitation and the role of the facilitator. Here, you find the responsibilities that person has towards the team that he/she is facilitating.

Chapter 3 is about organizing and designing collaborative spaces, focusing on the structure and physical space for the team meetings.

Chapter 4 introduces graphic tools that you can use when facilitating team conversations. Experts on the subject will share their experiences, recommendations, and learnings.

Chapter 5 focuses on the facilitation of collaborative processes. It will introduce a model of abstraction of a collaborative conversation, tools and techniques you can use in each stage and for different objectives.

Chapter 6 is fully oriented to facilitating the very beginning of an agile project. It will present important aspects to be taken into consideration, along with recommendations that lay the foundations of every agile project.

In **chapter 7**, you will find examples, techniques, tools and recommendations for facilitating the events within a sprint, such as its planning and facilitation of daily meetings, reviews and retrospectives.

Chapter 8 presents a model of skills development, and proposes a self-assessment model so you can check your performance and level of proficiency in which, to my understanding, makes an agile teams facilitator.

Without further ado, I invite you to enter the world of agile team facilitation. Let's go!

1

FACILITATION

Leonardo was my boss in one of my first jobs. The 2000s had just started, and I was taking my first steps in agility. At that moment, I knew how Extreme Programming (XP) worked as well as other approaches a little bit more isolated, but I didn't know about Scrum.

I also remember having come across facilitation, around that time, and failing to present Leonardo with the proposal of having a facilitator in one of the teams, due to not having a clear understanding of what it entailed.

As the years passed and my experience increased, I learned and refined my knowledge and understanding of facilitation and my role as facilitator.

FACILITATION

When an organization uses agile methodologies, in general, the teams work in a self-organized way and have a facilitative-leader.

The facilitator can be compared to a midwife, who assists in the process of creation but is not the producer of the end result (Bressen, 2005-2007).

> **Facilitation of groups**: *it is a process by which a person, who was chosen and accepted by all the group members, is substantively neutral and has no decision-making authority, who helps a group improve the way they identify and solve problems and make decisions, in order to increase its effectiveness. (Schwarz, 2002)*

This definition raises a paradox: the person who facilitates guides the process, and, therefore, is given authority. This authority delegated by the team and undertaken by the facilitator, sometimes, out of confusion is used to interfere with the result. This normally happens when the facilitator is also the leader of the team. It is for this reason that it is so important that when facilitating, we act with integrity and use this delegated authority exclusively to guide the process of conversation within the work team.

ALERT: THE DELEGATED AUTHORITY ASSUMED BY THE FACILITATOR, OFTEN DUE TO CONFUSION, IS USED TO INTERFERE WITH THE RESULT.

Facilitation is art, intuition, ability and science. Anyone can become a facilitator; he or she only need practice and attention.

Below, I'm inviting you to learn about the implementation of the principles of the facilitator based on the role of the facilitator.

RESPONSIBILITIES OF THE FACILITATOR

The main responsibility of the facilitator of an agile team is to foster an inclusive, safe, transparent and efficient communication process. This implies:

- To honor dialogue over monologue, foster the exchange of ideas and that group conversations maintain their sense.
- To help the team members implement and respect their agreements.
- To decompose big or complex topics into smaller, more manageable ones.
- To accompany the participants to navigate through conflict.
- To coordinate conversations, especially those with numerous participants.
- Paraphrase and help clarify when the contribution of a participant does not seem to be clear enough for the rest of the team.
- To make information and the decision-making process visible using flipcharts, posters, and drawings.
- To offer an adequate and trustful space and the required characteristics to carry out the work dynamics.
- To be aware of the participants emotions and the changes in the team's mood.

Based on my personal experience and practice as a facilitator, I have identified other responsibilities that I will explain below.

ANTICIPATING

The responsibility of the facilitator starts long before the beginning of the meetings or events of the team that is to be facilitated.

When I look back on my past experiences I admit I have achieved better results those times when I was prepared than when I wasn't. Although there are some teams of people who do not need a meeting agenda with anticipation, it is not always the case.

There are some teams which need to know the topics, the order, the duration, who the lecturer will be in each case, and which is the objective of each topic, to name a few requirements. Therefore, it is important to have everything the team needs and if you don't know, you can always ask.

I recommend warm-up activities with the team such as: interviews, readings, research, etc. The goal of these activities is to create connections among the participants, with the information and the topics they are going to cover.

If the topics can generate controversy, it is advisable to maintain a previous meeting with the members of the team to know their expectations and the extent of the possible opposing views.

Part of that high-level planning implies the identification of possible dynamics to use in each of the topics. Further ahead, I will present different types of dynamics which can be used in the meetings you facilitate.

As much as I believe in the importance of preparation, I also believe that it is more important not to attach yourself to the plan you have in mind. The plan is not valuable. What is valuable is the activity carried out previously when planning the facilitation. The plan only gives you the possibility to have a place

35

to go back to. We don't know if it is a safe place but, at least, it is a reference in case the process becomes chaotic.

> *It is not the plan that is important, it is the planning.*
> Dr. Graeme Edwards

ENSURING CONDITIONS AND RESOURCES

Facilitating a meeting is not only arriving and making sure a valuable conversation is under way. It is very important that this conversation takes place in a comfortable environment.

Anticipation also involves making sure that the place you are going to use is available and ready to be used. This avoids the awkwardness caused by arriving to the room and finding it dirty or being used by other people.

A nice temperature and good lighting are important factors. For example, natural light is much better than artificial light. In my experience, I have verified an exception to this rule: if the meeting is immediately after the lunch break, solar light has a strong drowsiness effect on the participants, much stronger than artificial light.

Although all teams are different and the contents of the agenda and the dynamics also have a strong effect, it is important to consider environmental aspects such as light and temperature and test them before the meeting.

A little piece of advice, which always applies, and which is especially effective in these cases, consists of keeping the participants in motion, with different activities, or simply by doing muscle stretching at regular intervals.

> *Physical exercise increases oxygen flow to the brain (...) an increase in oxygen is always accompanied by an increase in mental quickness. Dr. John Medina*[7]

The conversations that go beyond verbal add much more value. Writing, drawing and putting the body in motion becomes a great help. In order to do this, you need to use flipcharts, markers, posters, sticky notes as well as a wide space.

There is nothing less motivating than when having significant conversations than a reduced space, where it is only possible to speak due to the lack of additional resources.

Serving the team

The role of the facilitator of the team gives you power and at the same time, it takes it from you.

It gives you the power to intervene in the process as well as in the emotions of the conversations. At the same time, it takes away the power to intervene in the content. Therefore, from my point of view, it is important for the facilitator not to be a member of the team.

If the facilitator is part of the team and wants to intervene in the content, there is the alternative to explicitly express the change of roles before doing so, and then, after the intervention finishes, announce his/her return to the role of facilitator.

---

[7] Director of the *Brain Center for Applied Learning Research at Seattle Pacific University.*

Personally, I haven't had good experiences in these cases and recommend that if you see yourself going in and out of the facilitator's role several times, you delegate the facilitation to another person and get involved as a participant interested in the content.

Listening impartially

In Agility, every meeting is a participative decision-making conversation. By then end of the meeting, a decision, a commitment or an agreement will have been made, a result built collectively where each member has contributed in a small part. In this building process, you will find incomplete as well as more complete parts. More rounded ideas as well as crazy ideas. What can not be missing is the fuel of the result: ideas to debate and explore. Therefore, it is important that each member participates and contributes, including those who believe that contributing doesn't add value.

An important part of the facilitator's responsibility is to generate a conversation in which everyone feels heard and express their ideas.

If a member of the team remains silent, we can ask ourselves: What is he/she thinking? Why is he/she not participating? How is he/she living the trust and security in this meeting?

The most direct solution in these cases is asking that person about their opinion. Although it is the most direct, it is not necessarily the best way to approach the situation, since the person may feel insecure and defensive.

Further ahead, I will present several alternatives to handle this situation more gently and less directly that I have tried and which I feel more comfortable with.

If a member of the team repeats the same idea several times, I tend to ask myself: What is missing for him/her to feel heard? I prefer to think that the people repeat their ideas over and over in the same meeting because they don't feel heard rather than because they want to annoy someone else.

It may happen that the person who repeats the same idea many times confuses the fact of being heard with the disagreement of the rest of the team regarding his/her idea. This is something that has happened to me in several occasions and I dealt with it as follows: I address the person directly, I give them my opinion of the process [not the person] because as facilitators we guard the process and take care of the people, relationships and conversation.

Impartiality is a characteristic that should be maintained during the facilitation process. The focus of the facilitator is the process, not the content. For this reason, the person who facilitates does not show preference for one idea over the other but helps the members of the team find the result by themselves.

NAVIGATING THE CONFLICT

Conflict, in general, emerges progressively. It can be observed through body posture, looks, gestures, breathing, the language used, etc.

The emotions I have been able to identify as early signs of a conflict, so far, are: frustration, fear, anger or intolerance. Frustration, for example, because they can't impose their idea o because they can't manage to understand another member of the team's idea; fear to be damaged by another person's proposal; anger, because the team does not accept my contribution, intolerance to other people's contributions. These are just some examples.

To navigate through the seas of conflict, something I learned from Carlos Peix[8] was the difference between discussions based on positions and those based on concerns. For example, a member of the team wants to adopt a new reporting mechanism of hours worked per task performed and another member of the same team may disagree with the obligation of reporting the hours invested in each task. If the conversation remains at the level of the different positions about the reporting mechanism, it will never progress beyond "I agree", "I don't agree", "I agree", "I don't agree".

It is possible to leave this kind of conversation focusing on the motivations and concerns of each member of the team involved. So, it becomes more simple to talk about the worries and concerns of the members who are afraid of being controlled and questioned about the hours dedicated to the different tasks and those concerns of those who value the possibility of invoicing each client according to the time invested in each task.

USING ALL THE SPACE

I used to think that going to a meeting meant being present to discuss something from an intellectual point of view, sitting at the table together with the rest of the participants. Talking was as simple as expressing my thoughts in words.

As time passed, I discovered alternative and more interesting ways to talk, not only from an intellectual point of view, but from the body language and an emotional point of view.

---

[8] Carlos Peix is one of my partners at Kleer. You can find him on Twitter under the username @carlospeix

Achieving those levels of conversation involves going beyond the mere fact of sitting down at a table to share thoughts. It will be necessary to use all the space and resources available in the room. Some alternatives to involve different aspects of each member in the conversations are:

- Use flipcharts, sticky notes, sheets of paper, tape.
- Encourage the participants to write, to stand up, to group sticky notes, to draw on the flipcharts.
- Organize groups of people standing, polls, debate mini-groups, personalize posters, crossed presentations, etc.

The body is a great representative of emotions. The fact that we can involve it in conversations helps the participants to perceive other teammate's emotions and to feel more comfortable expressing their own.

Therefore, the conversations leave the mere intellectual standpoint to encompass a much wider spectrum of possibilities.

Leaving Attractive Evidence

What percentage of meeting minutes have you read in your life? I must confess that I have read less than 10%. I find it extremely boring to read the minute of a meeting (not to mention writing it).

To me, visual evidence is more attractive. Two alternatives that are as valid as a meeting minute are:

- **Graphic recordings,** in general, they require more dedication. I have had few good experiences when facilitating and leaving a graphic recording at the same time, but it is a matter of trying and having your experience. That´s why, I suggest that if you are about to facilitate a conversation, invite

41

a graphic recorder who will assist you with the visual recordings.

- **Audiovisual recordings** is, in my opinion, much more viable and consists of inviting a participant or several, to make a video with the summary of the session. This is something we do very often at Kleer with our internal meetings. All the videos are uploaded to a common repository and are accessible to all the members of Kleer. This, also helps achieve more transparency and visibility in the organization.

Enterprise Agility and Facilitation

Enterprise agility needs a solid foundation formed by the people and the teams, so that they can sustain the flexibility and adaptation required to face this new agile context.

Agile teams are the stem cell of enterprise agility and are based on the model of facilitative-leadership.

Facilitation can be applied in many situations: in each meeting, to make decisions, to explore alternatives, in any group conversation where we want inclusion, respect and consensus to flourish, and in those situations where it is important for all opinions to be heard without losing sight of the shared objective.

In the following chapters, I will share different approaches, techniques and tools for facilitation. Towards the end, I will include application alternatives for these resources in the different meetings of an agile process.

Food for Thought

Take a few minutes and reflect upon the subject discussed in this chapter.

Below, I share some questions for you to ask yourself and answer if you want to.

1. What do you think your team expects from you as a facilitator?

2. In what way, does your facilitation affect the decisions of your team?

3. What do you do when you don't agree with an opinion or decision in a meeting you are facilitating?

4. How do you make sure you are being impartial regarding the opinions and decision alternatives?

5. How do you make sure others know you are being impartial?

6. Who defines the agenda in the team meetings you facilitate?

7. What format does the evidence of the meetings come in? Are they attractive? Does it fulfill its function?

8. How many times are you involved in content meetings within the teams you facilitate?

9. In case the previous answer was "one or more times", what could you do to minimize that amount?

2

DESIGN
&
STRUCTURE

To adopt Agile in a team that I was leading –and which had been taken as a pilot experience -, it was decided to start gradually and adopt the new way to work organically (Hiromoto). Based on this model, the first meeting I decided to facilitate was a retrospective of the team.

I took the first step long before this retrospective and consisted of leading an investigation of the context. As soon as I knew that the team I was leading would be the pilot project of this change, I decided to meet with Federico, my manager, and gather information on the expectations of the parties interested in this transformation which would take place in the company.

— *Hello Federico, do you have 15 or 20 minutes to chat about the expectations of the Agility pilot project?*

— *Yes, sure. Let's find a room available and we'll talk about it.*

Finding a room available was not an easy task in the Company we worked at, so Federico and I ventured to find a space we could use at that moment.

A while later, we found room 102, occupied by four people who, at that very moment, showed their intention to get out. It only took us to stand outside the door and wait, a culturally accepted practice in the Company, which meant, "I have reserved this room, and I'm waiting for you to leave". So, the occupants hurried and left the place. Now, neither Federico nor I had reserved the room, pretending so, was also a cultural practice accepted in the organization.

Inside room 102, I asked again:

— *Federico, who are the interested parties in this Agility pilot?*

— *The person who is interested the most is Roberto. He is convinced that our area is not responding efficiently to the internal as well as external demands of the business, so we are going to start from the inside.*

— *That's the reason why this team was chosen, then?*

— *Exactly, as you provide your services internally to HR and Pay-roll, Roberto thought it was a good first step, with little risk of exposure.*

— *And what does Roberto expect from us?*

— *Well, that you start working in an agile way.*

— *Ok, but that does not give me a lot of clues regarding his ex-pectations. What do you think about meeting with him?*

— *I think it's fine. I will find an opening in his agenda and I'll let you know.*

— *Done*

Federico and I were about to leave room 102 but as we reached the door, we saw other people standing there with the same attitude "we have reserved the room..." Neither of us believed that was true, but we were leaving, anyway.

The next day I had the meeting with Federico and Roberto. As it was to be expected in that Company, the Senior Managers had the moral obligation to begin meetings thanking the other participants for the good work that they are performing. Another cultural practice. And so, Roberto started by saying:

— *Federico, Martín, first of all, I would like to congratulate you on the work that you have been doing. The fact that you are in-volved in the Agility pilot speaks highly of your predisposition and commitment with our company. –he continued– Martín, Fed-erico told me that you had some questions about the pilot.*

— *That's right, Roberto. The first point I would like to clarify is, what is your time and scope expectation of the pilot? I mean, how long and how deep do you expect us to work with agile method-ologies?*

— Well, time is going to define the depth. To me, it is not particularly important the degree of agility you want to follow internally, what I would like to see is the results of having adopted a more agile way of working with the client in mind. As for the time, I would like it to be as soon as possible.

— Well — I said — We are going to start adopting Agility as soon as possible, that is, next week after we have had our retrospective meeting. But, as I understand it, adopting this methodology in an organic and progressive way, we are going to slowly increase the level of Agility of work gradually. It is not going to happen from one week to the next. On this point, I would be comfortable with knowing that we share our expectations.

At this point, Federico was beginning to get nervous. It was evident because he was rubbing his hands, his face was sweaty, and he wouldn't stop moving one of his legs, like a nervous tic. He knew that Roberto was not happy if his employees contradicted him, and I reported directly to Federico, who reported to Roberto, which made the situation significantly worse. So, he quickly added:

— I understand Martín, but it is very hasty to say that we are not going to adopt Agility in its full potential.

— No, that is not what I'm saying – I answered, aware of Federico's concern –. I don't mean we are not going to adopt Agility in its full potential; I mean that we are going to gradually increase the level. On the other hand, we may not need to do absolutely everything. It will be determined by the context, which we will adapt to, retrospective to retrospective.

— Yes, sure. – nodded Roberto, which made Federico feel a little bit more at ease- Is there any other point you would like to discuss? –he asked.

— Yes, indeed, there is something I would like to go through. Next week we are going to have our first retrospective meeting where we will explore possible improvements in our way of working. It

is possible that those improvements involve other members of the team exclusively and, it is also probable that some of them include people outside the team. To what extent can we influence the way they work outside our pilot project?

— For the time being let's try not to –said Roberto–, we know that we can run risks inside the project, but I would like to have the least possible impact on the outside.

I knew that if we didn't handle the changes that involved other areas it was possible for the results not to be attractive enough. Without beating around the bush, I mentioned it to Roberto and the tree of us agreed that in the event this kind of situation presented itself, we would evaluate its impact before carrying out any action.

This conversation gave me enough information. I knew how far I could pull the rope regarding the changes in the way the team worked.

After this meeting, I moved forward in the preparation of the agenda and the dynamics to use in the meeting.

One of the widely accepted techniques in retrospectives is to divide it into five different stages (Larsen & Derby, 2006):

1. Setting the stage.
2. Gather data.
3. Generate insights.
4. Decide what to do.
5. Closing the retrospective.

Based on this model, I designed the following tentative agenda:

10 min: Prepare the stage

Activity: Check-In

20 min: Gather data

Activity: 6x3x5

25 min: Generate insights

Activity: Filtering

20 min: Deciding what to do

Activity: Planning improvements

5min: Closing the retrospective

Activity: Acknowledgments

Bearing in mind the problems to find a room in this organization I made sure to make a real reservation: I chose 104, a big, comfortable room with enough space for 5 members of the team and I reserved it for two hours, from 2pm to 4pm.

DESIGNING A MEETING

As a facilitator, it is important to keep out of the result of the meeting, promoting, at the same time, an effective dynamic. Part of facilitating an effective meeting depends on its design.

Therefore, I recommend anticipating to the event that you are going to facilitate and making sure you go through the three fundamental aspects of the design of every facilitating session:

background research, the agenda with its dynamics and physical space.

Below, I will expand on each of these aspects.

Background Research

The goal of the background research is to make sure we identify the real needs of the team beforehand to design a meeting with activities focused on those needs.

If you work in close collaboration with the team, it is possible to know some of these requirements, if you don't, it is highly advisable to assess them beforehand.

For my research, I met with Federico and Roberto, the interested parties in the pilot project to adopt Agility. By doing so, I could identify their expectations, the tolerance they had about the transformation to be implemented and how far we could go with the changes.

Identify the real needs of the team beforehand and design a meeting with activities focused on those needs.

A complementary resource to group meetings and, which sometimes becomes vital, are individual meetings with the members of the team. In these meetings, we can identify underlying needs, besides creating trust relationships with the people.

Another method, which can be used with big groups, is online interviews. They are somewhat less effective than face-to-face meetings, but they allow you to have meetings with many people in a short period of time. If the team is big (more than 20 people) and/or is geographically scattered, an additional resource can be online surveys.

MEETING THE EXPERTS

JUAN GABARDINI

Juan Gabardini is an Electrical Engineer and Informations Systems Licensee from the University of Buenos Aires (UBA), Agile Coach & Trainer at Kleer, professor at UBA and UNTREF.

🐦 *@jgabardini*

The beginning of a meeting

Have you ever been in a meeting where everyone looks at each other's face, expecting someone to start talking and don't even know why they are there?

Meetings have a purpose although, sometimes, it is not explicit. We meet to make decisions, to share information, to celebrate, to have fun.

How does the purpose emerge?

A person or a group take the initiative. These initiators want to achieve something and design the meeting as a strategy to do so.

When the objective is clear, it is possible to design the meeting. For example, positioning ourselves in the desired future towards the present, we analyze and design: What do we want to achieve -objective-? What would be the change produced by the meeting which will make us closer to the goal? How do we know, at the end of the meeting, that the meeting will achieve the desired changes? What dynamics or activities have we carried out to meet them? When have we performed each activity and how long did they last? Who did we invite to participate? How did we invite them to make sure they attend?

The invitation to a meeting

Did the key people come?

"In this meeting, we cannot make decisions because the key people did not show up." We looked at the organizer, and he answered: "But I did send them the invitation e-mail!"

An e-mail may be enough for some people, especially, for meetings that are already established, and have a constant rhythm.

However, in many cases, a little more than an invitation is required, for example:

- **Include RSVP in the invitation**. It is a request for the members invited to respond if they will attend the meeting. The letters are the acronym derived from the French expression Répondez s'il vous plaît, which literally means, "Please, respond".

- **Additional contact if any of the members didn't respond**: "Have you received the invitation? Are you coming?" This communication is more efficient if done in person than by e-mail. When this is not possible, it can be done on the phone, chat or e-mail, in decreasing order of effectiveness.

- **Personalize**. Adequate the invitation to each recipient: "You can bring a lot to the table because ..." or "It could be useful for you to come since..."

- **Adapt and adjust the possibilities of their participation**: "If you can't come for one hour, can you make it for 30 min? What background information do you need before deciding to attend?"

Previous contact

Between the invitation and the meeting, there is the possibility to do *nemawashi*, which is a Japanese word that refers to the action and technique used for transplanting trees successfully.

In the context of ideas and decisions, *nemawashi* means to explain the idea in advance to each participant, listening to their suggestions and concerns, and adapting the proposal to what was heard.

When we do the necessary *nemawashi*, all the members come to the meeting aware of the new ideas, they have had time to evaluate the impact of the proposal and their concerns have been taken into consideration. In those cases, the meeting is, above all, to formalize the joint agreement.

AGENDA AND DYNAMICS

Beginning the facilitation of a meeting without a well-established agenda can turn out to be a success or a failure. I have witnessed and participated in both.

It can be a success for those who feel very comfortable with improvisation and whatever emerges from these kind of situations and a failure when things don't turn out as the participants expected.

My recommendation is to always have an agenda and then modify it according to the needs of the moment. This agenda allows you to use it as a reference to go back to if things are not going as planned.

During this meeting, there are certain dynamics or activities that are possible to carry out at different moments and with different intentions. We'll discuss some of them briefly, and I will reference some others at the end of this chapter.

My proposal is that you use the resources and dynamics you consider adequate to design a tentative agenda for the meeting.

DON'T FOLLOW THE AGENDA TO A "T", USE IT AS A REFERENCE TO GO BACK TO IF THINGS ARE NOT GOING AS PLANNED.

If you have some time before the meeting, you can share the agenda with the participants in advance and, use it to obtain their feedback. With an agreed meeting agenda, it is very likely that the people will feel comfortable and keep to it.

When you don't have enough time in advance, the recommendation is to leave a few minutes at the beginning of the meeting to agree on the agenda. In that case, you present the topics proposed and come to an agreement at that moment.

PHYSICAL SPACE

The physical space is critical to help the participants of the session focus.

Part of the facilitator's job is to arrive earlier to the meeting place and make sure that:

- The chairs and tables are set in a certain way to foster interaction.

- All the necessary materials are available, such as board markers, flipcharts, and sticky notes.

- All the audio and video equipment is working correctly, as needed.

- The temperature is adequate.

AS A FACILITATOR, PART OF YOUR JOB IS TO ARRIVE EARLIER TO THE MEETING PLACE.

RESOURCES TO ORGANIZE MEETINGS

The resources to organize meetings help maintain its flow and dynamics, make the agenda visible, agree on activities, etc. Below, I will present some resources, which can be useful when facilitating a meeting.

CLEAR GOAL

To begin a meeting without having a clear goal can lead the conversation of the participants to branch out which will end up being a waste of time. If this situation is typical for the team, you can use this resource which helps clarify and explicit the objective of a meeting, so that it is a reminder for the whole group for as long as the meeting lasts.

MAKE THE GOAL OF THE MEETING EXPLICIT, AS A REFERENCE TO AVOID BRANCHING OUT AND WASTING TIME.

The agreed goal among the participants has more power and is more legitimate than a goal established by an external person. For the group to agree on the meeting goal you can ask the following questions:

- What would we like to achieve in this meeting?

- What do you want to take with you at the end of this meeting?
- What is the purpose of meeting and talking today?

I suggest you record and make the result of this first conversation visible so that it can be used as a reference to the participants, especially in the cases in which they lose sight of the meeting goal.

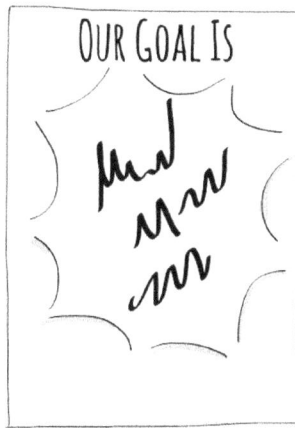

THE GOAL HAS MORE POWER AND IS MORE LEGITIMATE WHEN IT IS AGREED ON AMONG ALL THE PARTICIPANTS.

GROUP AGREEMENT

One of the meetings I like the least is the homeowners meeting. Fortunately, I haven't participated in one of these meetings in a long time. But when I did, all my energy remained evaporated at that meeting place. Shouting, disrespect, ungratefulness, indifference, a whole universe of personal aggression, which turned these meetings into a black hole that sucked all possibility of joint construction and made it disappear entirely.

To avoid these kind of situations, you can use group agreements. It is a very useful resource to initiate a meeting with high energy and maintain its quality throughout. It can yield great results if the team itself generates the agreement and if it is focused on how the members want to behave to take full advantage of the time allotted for the meeting in an efficient and respectful manner.

It is important to highlight the fact that the agreement has to be generated by the team and not by the facilitator. As a participant in a meeting, I feel much more identified with an agreement which takes my interests into consideration and has my mark rather than with an agreement imposed by an external party.

Having a group agreement helps the facilitator a lot, especially in the most challenging or conflictive moments of the meeting.

Depending on the nature of the meeting and the amount of time assigned, there is a wide variety of activities to create group agreements. One, which is very effective and can be solved in 15/20 minutes, is the following:

1. Draw two columns on a flipchart with the words: 'make sure' and 'avoid'.

2. Ask the participants to take 5 minutes to write those things that they must make sure and those that are important to avoid on sticky notes, so during the meeting, each person feels respected, secure and interested in collaborating with each other.
3. When the 5 minutes are up, invite them to stick their notes in the right columns and create associations based on similarities.
4. Finally, among all the participants, choose a common phrase or concept which identifies each set of notes grouped based on similarities.

Once the group has accepted the agreement, it is important to put it in a visible place in the room so you can make reference to it during the meeting.

It is important for the new people who come to the meeting and who did not participate in the agreement, to be familiar with it, and accept to respect it before making their participation effective.

ONCE THE GROUP AGREEMENT HAS BEEN ACCEPTED, IT IS IMPORTANT IT REMAINS IN A VISIBLE PLACE THROUGHOUT THE MEETING.

Panel of Activities

I remember a meeting I participated in, which was facilitated by a manager. It had only been 15 minutes and we didn't know how many topics we had discussed or how many we still needed to cover. The only thing that was clear was the hurry and a certain anxiety from the facilitator not to take longer than necessary with what we were discussing and move on to the next subject.

If the facilitator is the only one worried about the time and the topics of the meeting, it is likely because the participants do not understand the agenda or the progress of the topics clearly.

To avoid this, you can use a panel of activities, which is a resource that generates visibility of the structure and activities planned, as well as the progress of the agenda.

For example, if you need to discuss three important subjects in a one-hour-and-a-half meeting: the first two are mainly informative, and the third one involves making a decision. The agenda could be something like this:

1. *Check-In* (5 min)
2. Establishing goals (10 min)
3. Information topic 1 (10 min)
4. Information topic 2 (10 min)
5. Decision making (45 min total)
    a. Contextualization (5 min)
    b. *Brainstorming* (10 min)
    c. Understanding (15 min)
    d. Action plan (15 min)
6. Assessment of the meeting (10 min)

The proposal is to present this agenda in a visible, clear and explicit way. To do so, you can use a wall in the room where you can draw three columns with masking tape. Each of the columns corresponds to:

1. Pending Activities or To Do.

2. Activities in Progress or WIP (Work in Progress).

3. Finished Activities or Done.

The sticky notes are used to record each of the activities in the agenda and, at the beginning, are put in the column *Pending*.

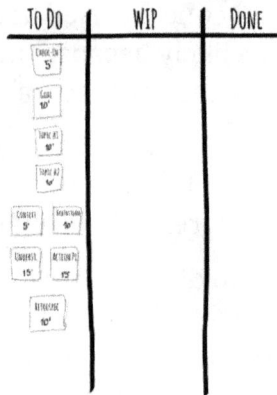

As the activities progress and complete, the post-it notes are moved from one column to the next, as appropriate. So, the process and progress of this meeting is visible all the time.

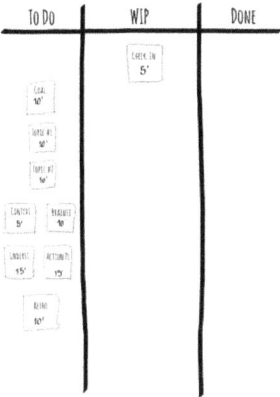

1. Beginning of the meeting

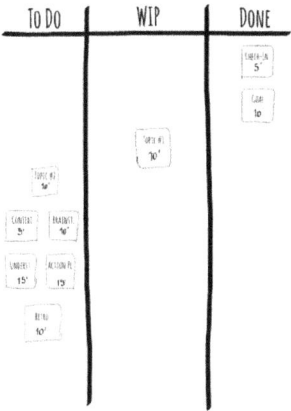

2. Towards half of the meeting

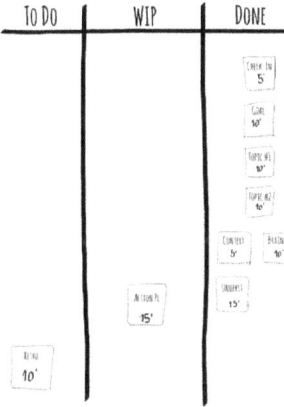

3. Towards the end of the meeting

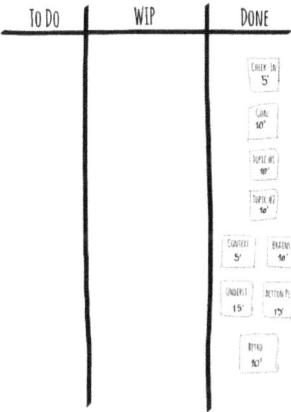

4. Meeting finished

Parking Lot

Once, I had to facilitate a meeting where the following dialogue took place:

— *We need to analyze the impact of the change in lighting for low-energy light bulbs in the annual budget.*

— *We should be careful with the provider we choose because we have had bad experiences.*

— *Well, yes, but now let's analyze the impact on the budget.*

— *So, are going to buy cold white or warm low energy light bulbs*

— *Does it affect the cost?*

— *No, I think they cost the same.*

— *So, let's analyze the impact on the budget.*

— *But... what are we going to do with the light bulbs we remove?*

— *...*

Many times, subjects emerge from the conversations that have little or nothing to do with the topic we are discussing at that moment or that imply a different level to the current one, for example: are more detailed or more strategic.

In this cases, for people not to feel ignored when putting forward new ideas or doubts, the emerging topics can be captured in the Parking Lot. Topics posted in the Parking Lot indicates that they will be discussed further ahead.

Setting up the Parking Lot does not take a lot of time, in general it is solved by sticking a poster to a wall where you can add the ideas and doubts expressed on sticky notes.

A PARKING LOT IS ONLY USEFUL IF THE AGENDA OF THE MEETING CONTEMPLATES SOME TIME TO DEAL WITH THE ITEMS DETAILED THERE.

It is probable that when the time comes to review the Parking Lot, the amount of topics is so big that there is no way you can discuss them all. In that case, something that can be useful to use time efficiently is to ask the participants to vote the items according to their priority and, then, deal with them from the most important to the least, discussing as many items as the time available allows.

Visible Stopwatch

There are some meetings where time flies. It happens to me all the time. In many of the teams I facilitate we go into the conversations so deeply and passionately that we lose track of time. Its consequence? The time is not enough or, expressed in a more responsible way, we do not use time efficiently enough.

A visible stopwatch can make a huge difference in these these kind of situations. There are physical ones (analog as well as digital) and virtual, applications which you can have on tablets or smartphones.

Having a visible stopwatch gives you a permanent temporal reference; it helps with self-organization of time and decision-making of how to use it in our conversations.

From my experience with stopwatches, I recommend:

- *Time Timer*, analog, in different sizes.
- *Liquid Timer*, analog, oil in water.
- *Marathon Timers*, digital, some come with big screens.
- *Lightningtalk Timer*, an app for iPad and iPhone
- *Stopwatch & Timer*, an app for Android

- *online-stopwatch.com*, works on any browser.

SILENCE SIGNAL

When the energy of the meeting and the conversation rise, it can be quite challenging to regain the attention of the participants. In this case, it is useful to have some sort of agreement to do so.

A very commonly used resource in these cases is known as the Silence Signal. It came about as a dynamic in the first years of primary school, and teachers use it to regain the attention of the group. It is also frequently used by facilitators since it is highly effective in meetings where there are a lot of participants.

The Silence Signal consists of inviting the participants to behave in a certain way (in this case, to be silent) when the facilitator does a certain signal. This signal, in general, is raising his/her arm. Therefore, when the facilitator raises the arm, extending his/her hand towards the ceiling and in silence, the participants imitate the facilitator, extending their arm to the ceiling and being silent at the same time.

Once all the participants are silent, it is possible to recover the attention of the group; only at that moment, does the facilitator lower his/her arm and continues with the activity.

It may happen that not everyone raises his or her arms. The important thing is to remember that the objective is to recover their attention and not that everyone raises their arms.

The goal of the silence signal is to regain their attention.

A complement of the Silence Signal is to add a sound or do a countdown. For example, to count from three to zero in a loud voice: THREE, TWO, ONE, ZERO! And, then, raise your arm.

Closing and Saying Goodbye

The meeting came to an end, and we looked at each other's faces. We felt a little bit uncomfortable, no knowing what to do. So, someone said "Well", and others said "Right", "See you" and we all hurried out of the meeting.

Who has not had the feeling of not knowing what to do at the end of the meeting? Does the meeting finish or doesn't it? How do we go on? What do we do?

Thus, it is important to give enough entity to the closure. There are many activities which can be done to close the meeting.

One activity which, according to my experience works very well, is the round of acknowledgments: each participant thanks the rest of the people for some action of the immediate past or meeting itself which contributed to his/her work or life.

All the resources that I have presented you with in this chapter are mainly to design and provide structure to the meetings. In the following chapters I will provide new resources that apply to other aspects of the interaction with people, such as, collaboration, participation and decision-making.

Food for Thought

Take a few minutes and reflect on the topic discussed in this chapter.

Below, I share a few questions to ask yourself and if you want you can answer.

1. Think about the last meeting you participated in. Do you think you could have improved something if you had prepared in advance? What?

2. ¿How often do you prepare the meetings you facilitate?

3. In case it is not often, what do you think it is stopping you? What would help you to turn preparation into a habit?

4. The meetings you facilitate; do they have a goal that is known to all? In case they don't, what do you think you gain from making it explicit and communicating it?

5. In case the objective of the meetings you facilitate is not known to all; what are the most important factors that, from our perspective, prevent you from making it visible and achieving an agreement about it?

6. *What, who, how could help you with these aspects?*

7. *How satisfied are you with the use of time in the meetings you facilitate?*

a. *Satisfied*
b. *Partially Satisfied*
c. *Dissatisfied*

If you are not satisfied, what is making you uncomfortable regarding the use of time in the meetings you facilitate?

8. How could the use of a meeting agenda help you?

9. How attractive are the records of the meetings you facilitate?

3

GRAPHICS

I have a proposal for you: imagine an elephant.

Now, imagine an elephant walking down the street. At the end of that road, on the horizon, there is a mountain, and at the top of the mountain, there is a windmill.

Although I don't know how you imagined that situation, the probabilities that you did it visually are high. Why? Because there are studies that show that between 60% and 65% of the world population process words visually (Deza & Deza, 2009).

In this chapter, we will discuss two expression and visual communication tools for groups: graphic recording and graphic facilitation. By using them, we significantly increase the creation of agreements, understanding of intentions, retention, and communication of the facts.

You will also find the testimony of experts in graphic facilitation who share their knowledge and experience with us.

MEETING THE EXPERTS
PABLO TORTORELLA

Pablo Tortorella is an Information Systems Engineer from the University of Buenos Aires (UBA), agile coach & trainer at Kleer, teacher at UBA and UNTREF and graphic facilitator.

🐦 *@pablitux*

I have had memorable experiences, which make me value and practice graphic facilitation and sketchnoting on a daily basis, at meetings as well as in classes, and academic and community events. An experience I remember is my students at the university fascinated by the topics of the subject exposed in colorful posters done live with markers and pastels on paper or with chalk on the blackboard. They were so excited that instead of going to their break, they stayed taking pictures and chatting around the illustrations.

Another experience is the one I had with highly motivated professionals when they saw that what they expressed during a meeting at their company was reproduced in images at the same time. On that occasion, they reached agreements and decisions on critical and complex issues in shorter periods than usual. They were surprised to see how well they had understood each other thanks to, in their words, *"Pablitux' graphic minutes"*.

We have also saved a lot of time on private and public courses and events by hanging the posters on the wall created over 4 hours and even 40 hours, making all the concepts discussed visible, as well as the results of the activities and the dynamics carried out. The posters on sight contributed to making quick references to previous moments and add conceptual updates in a matter of seconds by only crossing the classroom and pointing to the graphic in question.

We usually remember much better what we have seen create live or what we wrote down or created with our own hands, as opposed to using a slides presentation that's full of text or a lecture which only remains in the air. That's why I recommend the use of these visual techniques that are participative in the contexts that each person considers appropriate and, thus, promotes the understanding of complex issues and the exchange of opinions and information coming from multiple sources.

Graphic Recording

Graphic recording is the practice by which conversations translate into images. Typically, it can be done in two ways:

1. **Private** *(Sketchnoting)*: takes visual and individual notes at meetings and conferences.
2. **Public** *(Graphic Recording)*: takes visual notes for one or more people and they are visible by a lot of people, at meetings and conferences. In general, it is done on large sheets of paper hung on the wall. In this case, it can be used as an excellent resource to involve participants in a meeting.

When graphic recording is done publically, it maximizes the involvement of the participants in a meeting. Since this is what we are after, as agile facilitators, I'll show you this tool:

Whenever someone is speaking, there will be people listening. Well, almost always. People can be listening or pretending to listen while they think about they are going to say next, or even worse, about something else entirely disconnected from the subject of the meeting, for example, their upcoming vacations, moving out, their new car or about how tight their shoes are. This distraction creates and abyss between the person talking and the people pretending to listen.

When a graphic recorder completes posters with images that represent what is being discussed, the participants get involved in a different and more active way in the conversations. The person who speaks, can at the same time, see in real time the interpretation of what he/she is saying.

Therefore, you create a visual representation of all the meeting, which validates the different points of view and generates synthesized and attractive evidence of what happened. This evidence can be used as traditional minutes. To do that, you can take photos of the final drawing and send it via e-mail, print it in a poster format and hand it out to the participants.

MEETING THE EXPERTS

CLAUDIA SANDOVAL

She is known as the Graphic Facilitation Fairy. She co-facilitates and visually records meetings all around Latin America. In the agility environment, Claudia is co-founder of Kleer in Colombia and she is a member of the agile community there, where she participates voluntarily by sharing her talent.

🐦 *@claumsandoval*

Dear Agile team facilitator apprentice:

My biggest learning achievement in the last three years is that when we combine the facilitation with drawing, we are opening the door to vindicate the inner child, that child who is usually hidden or forgotten in our memories and that, at the same time, influences many of our decisions.

To illustrate what I mean with "vindicate" set yourself inside the movie Ratatouille, when Anton Ego —the food critic- goes to Chef Gusteau's restaurant and is served his favorite childhood dish.

¿Remember?

Anton connects with the most significant moments of that time and everything inside him changes, revitalizes.

I think that when we make people draw, when we show them an illustrated summary and communicate our ideas with doodles, we are connecting with that child we once were.

Today, I see that reunion as a door to ingenuity and, thus, to vulnerability which, as investigator Brené Brown explains, is the place where all our most significant interactions occur. That is, the place where you, as a facilitator, can be the catalyzer in an agile team, creating and fostering significant interactions where the magic – the co-creation- emerges.

And, why is all this important?

Because as facilitators and graphic recorders we strive to make the invisible visible, and that is only achieved from the heart. As the Little Prince said: "It is only with the heart that one can see rightly; what is essential is invisible to the eye."

Now, as I imagine that what you were expecting is an *expert's* contribution about the technique, here it is:

As a graphic recorder my focus is on how to distill and connect, which means, on cooling the steam of a conversation to find and draw the essence of what is trying to emerge from there, to see how the dots connect and, so, create a visible map of what is going on in that interaction.

Personally, I only feel that the distillation and connection are possible after cultivating, deliberately and constantly, an ability: the ability to listen.

This systematic practice has produced a remarkable difference in my work this year. The last twelve months I have listened to draw and drawn to listen. That simple: in any context, with one person, a hundred or more people speaking, I automatically prepare a blank sheet of paper, markers, and *voilà*, my brain starts to activate, and the images begin to flow. So I make peace with my inner little girl and critic and, slowly but steadily, proceed to doodle.

Now, I want to make clear that my context for the drawing is usually a delicate channel, which means, that my attention is exclusively focused on listening, that is why I emphasize its importance. However, I imagine that as an agile team facilitator apprentice your aspiration is to talk and draw simultaneously. If this is the case, the first thing to remember is, Do not despair! Take your time to think and practice the drawings you will use in your interventions until they come to you easily and quickly.

Remember: make it simple, and "quick like a bunny", as Brandy Agerbeck says. It is not about art but about understanding the world through simple drawings.

Fairy Secret: Prepare some posters, sketching the most important drawings with a yellow marker on white paper and during your presentation focus on the discourse and on repainting with dark colors what you drew in yellow. To get more advice on this ask Pablitux or Pat Molla, they do a wonderful job.

To sum up, a good facilitator could ask himself: if by recording graphically we act as distillers or filters who extract the essence of what is being said, what happens with what does not go through the filters, along with the non-essential?

This question has been part of my most recent exploration, and I have found that, indeed, when I finish my recording session of the day, part of that invisibility exists and is flowing inside me, transforming into symptoms that are similar to a hangover the following day.

For this, I have found certain practices such as meditation, which helps me let it flow with a particular intention, take the load off and find the balance.

My suggestion is not that you meditate, but that you are aware of your mind and body, and explore different alternatives to help you relax and be more present.

Hope you have the best drawing moments.

Fairy

http://claumsandoval.tumblr.com/

Graphic Elements

There are many elements you can use and combine when creating visual recordings. Let's revise them, along with the tips and practices shared by Claudia "Fairy" Sandoval.

Text

It is important to represent the text fast and legibly. Different letter sizes represent various levels of information or importance of the ideas. It is usual to write everything in capital letters for the titles and lower case for the contents.

ABC
abc

Exercise your capital letters:

THE QUICK BROWN FOX JUMPS OVER THE LAZY DOG

Fast:

_____

_____

_____

Legible:

_____

_____

_____

Fast and legible:

_____

_____

_____

Exercise you lower case letter:

Grumpy wizards make toxic brew for the evil queen and Jack

Fast:

_____

_____

_____

Legible:

_____

_____

_____

Fast and legible:

_____

_____

_____

Vignettes

Vignettes group text, provide order and clarity. The easiest and fastest to draw, the better. It is important to make sure they are legible from a distance.

Lines

Lines relate elements and express the degree of connection between them. Thick lines indicate strong relationships. Thin or dotted lines represent weak connections.

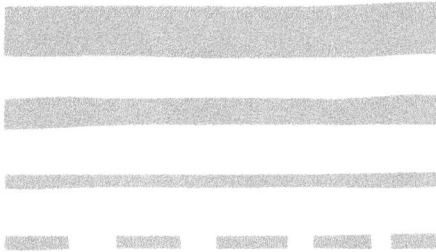

ARROWS

Arrows order the reading. They represent flows and processes and can also be used to indicate action.

BOXES

Boxes can be used to point to places and emphasize certain parts of the discourse. They also group elements, such as vignettes and highlight them.

A recommendation is first to write the text and then to draw the box that contains it; this is to avoid drawing a small box and having to compress the text. Another piece of advice is to use darker colors for the text and lighter for the boxes.

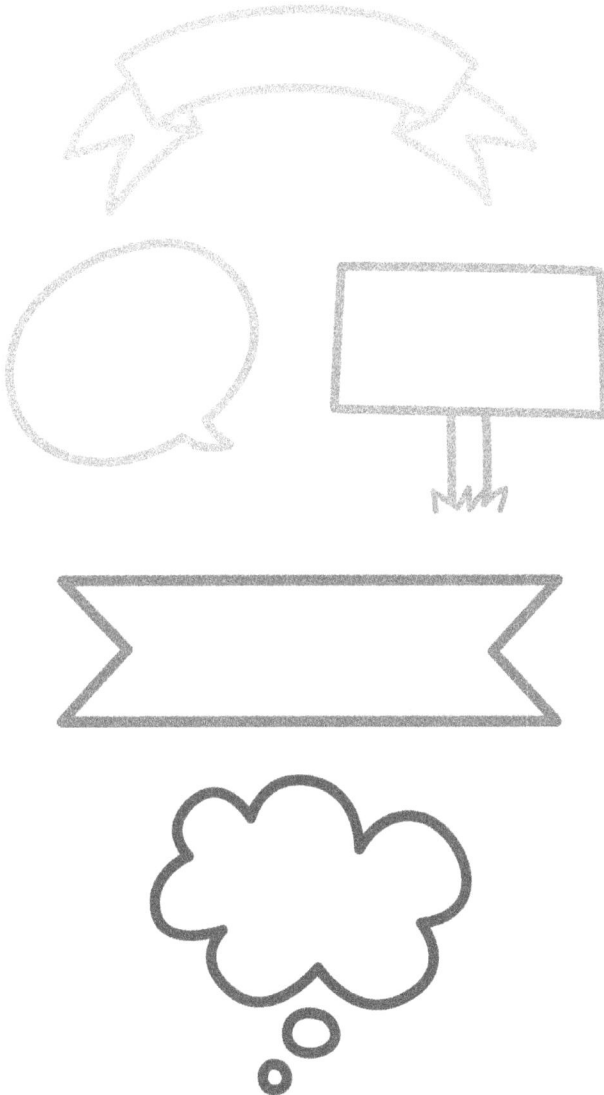

SYMBOLS

Symbols contextualize places as well as dates and usually emerge from the group language.

Effects

Effects, such as shadows and sparkle can be used to highlight the elements drawn, energize them or emphasize them.

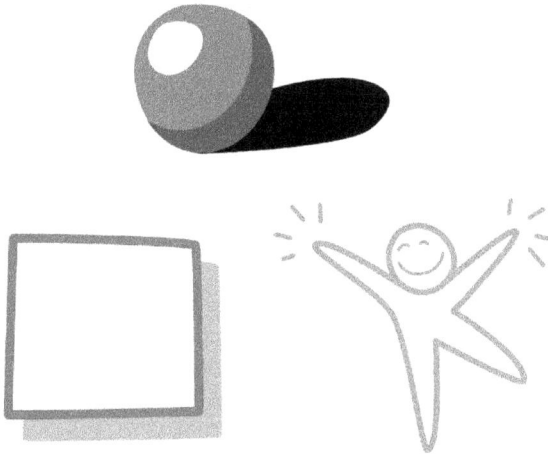

CAREFUL: it is important to be consistent in the use of shadows and make them all towards the same side.

PRACTICE

Now, you can do some of the exercises shared by the Fairy.

The first exercise consists of drawing people. To discover them, you only need to connect the dots in the following graphics:

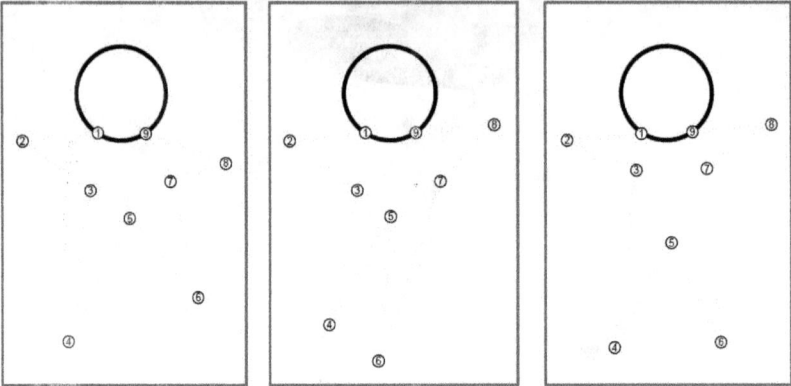

In this second exercise, find a team of people. In order to do this, draw over the lines:

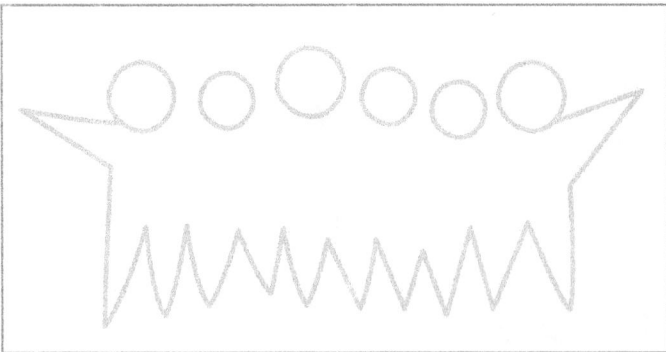

Now, copy the images of the people freehand. You can try twice with each picture.

NOTE: If you are reading the digital version of this book, try to make the drawings on a piece of paper.

Graphic Facilitation

We could say that graphic facilitation is the evolution of graphic recording.

A graphic facilitator does not only record conversations using images, but he/she also intervenes in the participative and collaborative process of a group of people to help them achieve a concrete goal.

I have invited Zulma Patarroyo, who is an international expert on the subject, to shed some more light on the differences and similarities between graphic recording and facilitation.

Meeting the Experts

Zulma Patarroyo

Founder and director of PATALETA, a facilitation and graphic recording company. Zulma has several years of international experience in design and facilitation of learning processes at organizations of different sectors.

@PataletaNet

Graphic recording? Graphic facilitation? Are they the same? Are they different? Who cares...

In my experience as recorder and as a graphic facilitator, I have found different definitions.

My definition has also changed over time. At his moment, I think there is a progressive continuous between graphic recording and graphic facilitation. It is not so much that one contains the other, but rather that both complement and interact with each other. The recording can be included in the designs of the participative processes and, intentionally or not, can contribute to facilitating the learning process.

From my point of view, everything is related to the role of the person doing the job, the use given to these graphic tools and the level of involvement of the participants with the visual elements.

Graphic recording

In this case, the emphasis is on recording and creating a visual memory: an almost simultaneous translation of a text and images of the things others shared orally. If it happens within the framework of a workshop, the graphic recording takes place during the plenary sessions; if it is a seminar, conference, forum, panel or something of the sort, the graphic recording happens while the lecturer is doing his/her oral presentation. This is what is usual to see in many events where experts are invited to share their projects or experiences in a conference or panel format. In many cases, there is a graphic recorder who translates what is being said verbally into a visual synthesis, which, if possible, is exhibited at the same place of the event. Afterwards, these graphic memories are shared digitally, and in some cases, in print.

Although graphic recording has an impact on the way the participants listen and process the shared information, it invites deeper conversations and motivates them to continue exploring and learning. It is mainly something that graphically summarizes what others shared orally and which will remain as their visual memory.

Graphic recording is done on large size paper or digital supports, and the process of graphic synthesis is visible to all the participants.

There are some related practices, such as *sketchnotetaking* or graphic notes but, unlike graphic recording, they are done individually; the participants do not have access to them during the event.

To sum up:

- The person who **records graphically,** listens and produces a graphic synthesis.

- It is mainly **used** as a memory shared after an event and, in some cases; it is also exhibited during the event.

- The **participants** of the event are passive observers.

Graphic facilitation

In this case, the emphasis is on the facilitation, that is, as the visual tools are used intentionally in participative learning processes, dialogue and strategic planning, among others.

From my perspective, it is a mistake to use the word facilitation as a noun, like when someone says "that facilitation was excellent" referring to the graphic synthesis done on paper during a certain event. Facilitation is not a thing; it is an action.

Some examples of graphic facilitation are:

- The use of graphic tools intentionally to promote the participation of people, in general, in workshop spaces.

- The pre-design of visual metaphors to complete in front of a group and, to explain a theory, a story, a model or a concept.

- The pre-design of visual templates, so the participants through the use of this graphic tool can have an organized conversation, to come to agreements and see, in one single space, the project as a whole.

- The design of big size agendas in a workshop, explanatory boards, matrix recordings or harvest templates to facilitate the dialogue in methodologies such as Open Space, World Café or Pro-action Café.

- The use of a graphic documentation canvas (which we usually call *pataleta*) as a material for a conversation.

To sum up:

- The **graphic facilitator** designs and facilitates participative activities using graphic tools. One of the tools can be graphic recording, which is used in a team with someone in charge of recording. Other tools are large size or individual templates, boards, cards, etc.

- It **is used** for participative learning activities, strategic creation and planning, among others.

- The **participants** are active, interact with the graphic tools, produce a synthesis of the texts and, sometimes, based on images on graphic templates, they have conversations motivated by such images.

2. Take a pencil and make a drawing that reflects the previous text:

3. *What do you think about the image you just drew?*

4. *What do you think about yourself, how did you fell making the drawing?*

5. What do you feel if I ask you to show the drawing to the person who is now closest to you?

6. What do you think that person can say about your drawing?

7. If you dare, show it to that person and ask him/her what they think. Was there a difference between what you expected him/her to think and his/her real opinion?

8. How did you feel showing him/her your drawing?

9. Now, going back to you, how do you remember yourself drawing in your childhood?

10. How distant is your child artist from your adult artist? If they are too far apart, what do you attribute it to?

11. Identify an activity you can do with great skill. It can be a hobby, an instrument. How did you feel when you first started doing it?

12. How do you feel now when you see you have developed that skill?

13. What do you think of the learning process?

4

COLLABORATION

So far we have discussed topics such as facilitation, the role of the facilitator and the attitudes expected. We have also dealt with different tools that are useful to figure out the structure of a meeting as well to document what happens there in an engaging way.

A very important aspect of the facilitation of an agile team is the respect for the autonomy in the decision-making process of the work teams. Being aware of this aspect prevents us from meddling where we shouldn't, for example: getting involved in the conversations and influence or modify its content; giving orders instead of inviting; leading the decision-making process towards the results we deem convenient, etc.

To help promote autonomy in agile teams – the actual protagonists of the processes we facilitate-, in this chapter we will focus on **collaborative conversations** and review the practices and tools related to this topic which can be applied to facilitation.

FACILITATING COLLABORATIVE PROCESSES

One of the abilities that self-organized teams have is their ability to make decisions in a collaborative and autonomous way.

Since part of my job is dedicated to promoting these kind of spaces and dynamics within groups and teams, I have done quite a lot of research about it.

A few years ago, I came across a model, which I thought was extremely clear, called The Diamond of the Participatory Decision Making (Kaner, 2007).

Kaner identifies five stages – he calls them zones-, which form the diamond: [1] business-as-usual zone, [2] divergent zone, [3] groan zone, [4] convergent zone and [5] closure.

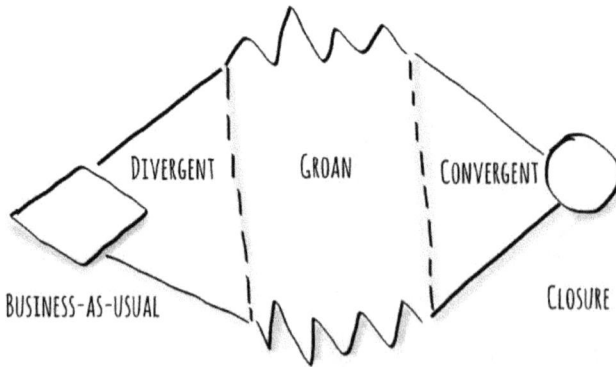

Once a challenge has arisen, the **business-as-usual zone** appears when the group finds a solution which is apparently obvious. As a facilitator, it is important to promote the participation of each person during this process. If you sense not everyone has participated in the conversation or that there is at least one person who disagrees with the result, help the group come out of the **business-as-usual zone** and move on to the **divergent zone**.

The **divergent zone** generates a different environment. This zone is for exploring, imagining, creating and sharing. Here, the challenge of the facilitator is to accompany the group in this exploration. It is vital to promote an environment of trust and transparency for the majority of the people to participate. It is important to minimize potential sensations of impossibility in the participants when sharing their different points of view.

Techniques such as *Brainstorming* and *BrainWriting* can be used in this zone to open the game to the diversity of ideas and proposals.

Once all the participants have expressed their ideas, it is very likely that some discomfort and anxieties arise and certain stress dominates the air. This is normal: welcome to the **groan zone**.

The role of the facilitator is key in this zone, especially to avoid the attempts of the group to avoid this moment or situation. It is important to guide them there and accompany them to navigate it. This is the zone of mutual understanding, of sharing and contrasting impressions, building shared meaning, understanding and listening to each other.

It is an uncomfortable, challenging zone, and it is quite possible that everyone wants to leave that zone as soon as possible. Don't hurry looking for a specific result, just breathe deeply, facilitate and accompany.

The **convergent zone** appears when the group starts to find its way and sees a light at the end of the tunnel. This is the zone where agreements are generated, enthusiasm and discussions are back, some ideas are discarded and others selected.

Towards the end, a decision must be made and it is also recommended that a plan of action is defined and accepted by everyone. This is the moment of **closure** of the diamond.

After this brief tour of the different zones of the Kaner Diamond, I invite you to explore a series of tools that can be helpful to you in the facilitation of each stage.

Tools for Participation

At the beginning of the diamond it is important to promote the participation of the people since they are entering the divergent zone. Below, I'll show you some tools to help you promote this participation.

Brainstorming

Brainstorming is a technique used to create a lot of ideas in a short period of time. It helps the team expand their thoughts to include ideas that cover all the dimensions of a problem or solution. In general, the amount of ideas is too big to act on them. Therefore, they must be filtered, prioritized and grouped in a collaborative way.

For a *Brainstorming* session to be effective, I suggest you pay attention to the following situations:

1. Avoid criticizing ideas.
2. Record each idea in a visible way, on a post-it note, on a *flipchart* or a whiteboard.
3. Check that everyone understands what the presenter of each idea is proposing.
4. Be careful that the ideation process does not take more time than agreed.

There are different ways of facilitating a *Brainstorming* session, some are more and some are less structured. Below, I'll walk you through some of the possible models.

1. Emerging *Brainstorming*

The facilitator invites the participants to share aloud the ideas that come to their mind while he records them on a *flipchart.*

This dynamics can last from 10 to 15 minutes. One limitation of this approach is that only extroverted members of the group will participate and the introverts, since they are more reserved with their ideas, will not participate in the process.

2. Guided *Brainstorming*

This dynamics involves adding a layer of structure to the *Brainstorming.* Based on the problem to solve or the question to answer, the facilitator invites the participants to write their ideas in silence and individually, on post-it notes or file cards. This way of recording avoids the participants to influence each other. The ideal duration of this process should be between 5 to 10 minutes.

IDEATION IN PARALLEL AND IN SILENCE AVOIDS THE PARTICIPANTS TO INFLUENCE EACH OTHER.

After the silent recording, each participant is asked to present just one idea until the round of people is complete. This process repeats until you have done as many rounds as the ideas the participants have.

Another possibility is that each participant presents all his or her ideas before moving on to the next. In that case, if a person has an idea that was already presented by another member, he or she can communicate it and write it on a post-it note next to the original idea, slightly superimposed to it or just write "+1" on the idea presented by the other participant.

124

3. Shifting *Brainstorming*

This variant of *Brainstorming* promotes physical and space movement.

The dynamics start by forming groups of four or five people distributed in workstations. Each station can have a *flipchart* on the table or stuck to the wall.

Each group has a fixed amount of time –between 5 to 10 minutes- to propose ideas on the topic that is being discussed and record them on their poster. When the time is up, the posters remain in the corresponding workstations and all the groups of people rotate stations. The groups find in their new workstations the posters with the ideas recorded by the previous group and have between 5 and 10 more minutes to add new ideas. The rotation repeats until each group returns to their initial workstation and finds their original poster full of new ideas. Finally, each group summarizes what they found and presents it.

As an alternative, each station can have a different topic, which promotes that all the participants can provide their vision as they rotate.

BrainWriting

BrainWriting (King, 1998) is an evolution of *Brainstorming*. A technique also known as 6-3-5. the name refers to the fact that the process has six rounds (6) with three ideas each (3), for five minutes each round (5).

For *BrainWriting* we use sheets of paper, which contain a blank space at the top, and a table of three columns by six rows. A sheet of paper is handed out per participant and they are invited to write a question which represents the challenge or the problematic for which they need to propose ideas, for example "How could we increase the level of satisfaction of our consulting clients?"

CHALLENGE:		
IDEA 1	IDEA 2	IDEA 3

As soon as the participants have written the questions, they have five minutes to propose three ideas in writing, in silence and individually, which will be written in the three cells of the first row of the table.

By the end of the five minutes, each participant passes their sheet of paper to the person next to him/her (it is useful to agree on a direction -left or right- and keep it until the end of the exercise), who will have another five minutes to propose three ideas in the following row of the table. These ideas can be inspired by the previous ones, widen the previous ones or they can be completely new.

The process continues until the sheet of paper has passed through six participants, who all in all will have completed the six rows of the table, with a total of 18 ideas.

At the end of the process, the participants share the ideas recorded on their sheets, eliminate duplicates and record them in a visible manner to everyone.

An alternative to the table with three columns by six rows is to use a sheet of paper with 18 post-it notes arranged in three columns and six rows. The ideas are written on the post-it notes and, at the end, are detached and organized to be shown.

In general, a *BrainWriting* process is followed by some sort of selection and prioritization process of the ideas in a collaborative manner.

Small Groups of People

There are some cases where big groups are not the best choice to debate and make decisions in a participative way. Some clear symptoms of this situations are: the lack of participation of many members, the use that a small amount of people make of their space to talk, several conversations in parallel, lack of attention, dispersion, etc.

In these cases, the big group can be divided into smaller groups, of between 4 and 6 people each. Unlike the big group, the small group promotes the participation; the parallel conversations are less usual, it generates a more intimate environment, people have more time to express themselves and they feel much less intimidated.

To Speak In Smaller Groups Allows More Time For Everyone To Express Themselves And Feel Much Less Inhibited.

A limitation of dividing the group into smaller groups is that conversations and their conclusions remain isolated inside each small group and are not visible to the outside. To avoid this situation, each small group can share the result of their conversations with the rest of the auditorium when the event closes. It is important for this procedure to be explicit from the beginning, so each small group chooses a person in charge of the report and of writing the summary of their conversation and the outcomes.

If this tool is used within the divergent zone of Kaner's Diamond, it is not necessary to look for consensus or give closure to every conversation because this zone is focused on opening possibilities.

Tools for the Conversation

There are different tools and techniques that can be used to promote collaborative conversations within a work team. Below, I share a few of them, which are possible to use in any zone of Kaner's Diamond, especially in the groan and convergent zones.

Equalizers

At the beginning of the 2000's, I had the chance to participate in the production line automation project of several fruit and vegetables packing plants in Southern Argentina. At the initial meeting, along with the interested parties, I remember that the main conversation focused on the relative importance of the scope (everything that had to be done), the schedule (specific dates according to European legislation and opportunities) and client satisfaction (the users of the production line). The talks took longer than expected and a lot of people had opinions that, at times, seemed contradictory: at one moment they thought something, and then they changed their minds for no apparent reason. At that meeting, we didn't quite reach a consensus and the future did not seem very clear. We were not surprised when, a few weeks after the beginning of the project there were some setbacks due to misunderstandings.

A few years later, between 2008 and 2009, I found myself in a similar situation working on a very similar project: they were the same objectives but on a tobacco production line.

This time I decided to change my approach to deal with the issue of the relative importance of the scope vs. the schedule vs.

the risks vs. customer satisfaction vs. the development team satisfaction.

Together with a co-facilitator, we stuck a big line with Scotch tape on the floor and proposed that that line was a slider (like the volume controls used in radio and TV in the 80's) to determine the importance of each aspect at a time. We established one of the extremes as the "High level of importance" and the opposite extreme as the "low level of importance".

The first assignment was to ask each person to stand in the part of the line they thought was correct to determine the scope's level of importance. Each person stood on different places and a conversation was generated until we reached consensus. Afterwards, we drew the line with the measurement agreed on a board and we moved on to the following topic in the schedule. We proceeded in the same way, and repeated until we covered all the aspects to evaluate in that meeting.

When we finished, the drawing in the board showed the consensus on the relative importance of each of the aspects discussed.

During the development of the project, this information was always available and referenced. So, a lot of misunderstandings and mistakes were avoided in the communication of the priorities.

This facilitation technique can be helpful for a group of people to discuss their positions and opinions on a particular topic.

The first step is to mark a physical or imaginary line (with tape or thread).

Then, explain the meaning of the extremes to the participants, for example: "I totally agree" and "I totally disagree".

Transform the topic of the debate into an affirmation, for example: "the scope of this Project is fixed" or "the schedule of this project cannot be altered under any circumstance". Ask the participants to stand in line according to their opinions regarding the affirmation.

Suggest conversations in pairs where, each participant tells the other person why he/she is standing in that part of the line. It is likely that they change their minds during the conversation.

Then, ask each pair to share their conclusions with the rest of the people and then help the group reach consensus on the place they will adopt regarding the affirmation in question.

AT THE END OF EACH TOPIC, HELP THE GROUP REACH CONSENSUS.

This equalization technique helps reach consensus on different topics and, at the same time, presents a challenge regarding attention and focus, since it can cause conversations to become very disperse.

FISHBOWL

Fishbowl is a conversation dynamics, which can be used to generate dialogue spaces on different topics in large groups.

At the beginning of the activity, four or five chairs are arranged in an inner circle. This circle is what is called fishbowl.

Outside this circle and a somewhat far away, arrange the rest of the chairs laid out in concentric circles, surrounding the main circle.

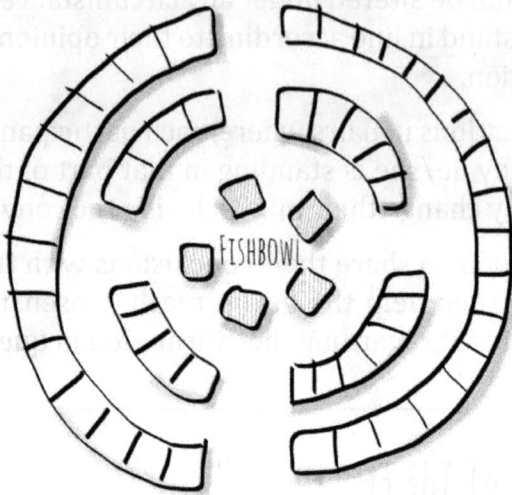

FISHBOWL

In this fishbowl is where the four or five people who want to initiate the dialogue will sit.

In case you facilitate an **open** fishbowl, it is important that one of the chairs is left empty. If you facilitate a **closed** fishbowl, all the chairs are filled.

The dynamic starts with the participants in the center who initiate a conversation of the topic to be discussed. The rest of the participants observe and listen in silence.

In an **open** fishbowl, any of the participants sitting in this external chairs can walk, sit on the empty chair, and participate in the conversation. As a chair should always be left empty, some of the people who were already participating in the conversation leaves voluntarily, leaving an empty chair so that, eventually, another person from the external circle takes that place. This movement repeats as many times as the participants want to participate and until the pre-established timeframe is up.

In a **closed** fishbowl, where there are no empty chairs in the main circle, the facilitator pre-establishes a specific timeframe for the participants to talk about the issue in question. At the end of that time, all the participants leave the main circle and new groups of participants occupy the chairs, repeating the cycle until completing the pre-established timeframe for the dynamic.

At the end of any of these fishbowl dynamics, the facilitator will summarize the topics and main points discussed. This dynamic can be accompanied by graphic recording.

World Café

At the beginning of 2009 I had the opportunity to facilitate a conversational process in a gourmet company. Unlike previous years – when only the owners of the company designed the gourmet offer-, this time they wanted to design the new offer (main courses, desserts, entrées, menus) in a collaborative way, together with the employees.

It was a group of 23 people including owners, waiters, cooks, chefs, administrative and cleaning staff. We started the day by dividing the participants in five small groups of four people each and one of three people. The groups were distributed in different tables of the restaurant and each table had a blank poster, markers and post-it notes.

We started a 20-minute-conversation where each small group had to answer the questions: *What inspires us in this job and pushes us forward?*

After 20 minutes, each group left a host at their table and the rest were arranged in the other tables, forming new groups.

In this second round, we allocated 20 minutes to talk and answer the question: *How do we think we can make a significant difference in our customer's experience?*

133

At the end of the second conversation, the participants – except the host – rotated tables again forming new groups. They spent the following 20 minutes answering the question: *What concrete changes would you make in our offer (entrées, main courses, desserts and menus) to guarantee a better experience for our customers?*

At the end of the three cycles of conversations, we shared our ideas and we agreed on the changes for the new offer of the restaurant.

This activity that I just described is an actual case where we applied the technique called *World Café,* which consists on arranging a large group of people in mini-groups of between 4-5 people each.

The place is decorated simulating a café where each table has a blank poster as tablecloth to promote the writing and the use of post-it notes.

Once the small groups have been formed, the conversations take place in three or more 20-minute cycles each. By the end of each cycle, the people move to other tables leaving a host at the table and they form new mini-groups.

Each conversation cycle is guided by a powerful question formulated especially for that occasion. Several cycles can use the same question.

At the end of the conversation cycles, the table hosts present, in a pre-established time-box, what they had been working on at their tables and then, once all the presentations have been heard, they move on to the moment of agreement and consensus. The final result can be captured in posters through graphic recording and videos and also uploaded to social networks.

AN ORGANIZATION OF EXPERTS

WORLD CAFÉ COMMUNITY FOUNDATION

The mission of the World Café Community Foundation is to transform the world for the benefit of all life through convening and supporting collaborative conversations world-wide.

🐦 *@TWCcommunity - http://www.theworldcafe.com*

The *World Café Community Foundation* recommends the following principles to design a good dynamic:

1) Set the Context

Pay attention to the reason you are bringing people together, and what they want to achieve. Knowing the purpose and parameters of your meeting enables you to consider and choose the most important elements to realize your goals, for example: what themes or questions will be most pertinent, what sorts of harvest will be more useful, etc.

2) Create a Hospitable Space

Café hosts around the world emphasize the power and importance of creating a safe and hospitable space. When people feel comfortable to be themselves, they do their most creative thinking, speaking, and listening. Therefore, it is important to consider how our invitation and the physical set-up contribute to creating a welcoming atmosphere.

3) Explore Questions that Matter

Knowledge emerges in response to compelling questions that are relevant to the real-life concerns of the group. Powerful questions help attract collective energy, insight, and action. Depending on the timeframe available and your objectives, at the World Café you may explore a single question or use a progressively deeper line of inquiry through several conversational rounds.

4) Encourage Everyone's Contribution

As leaders, we are increasingly aware of the importance of participation, but most people don't only want to participate, we also want to actively contribute to making a difference.

That is why it is important to encourage everyone to contribute their ideas and perspectives, while also allowing and receiving anyone who wants to participate by simply listening.

5) Connect Diverse Perspectives

The opportunity to move between tables, meet new people, actively contribute your thinking, and link the essence of their discoveries to ever-widening circles of thought is one of the distinguishing characteristics of the *World Café*. As participants carry key ideas or themes to new tables, they exchange perspectives, greatly enriching the possibility for surprising new insights.

6) Listen for Both: patterns and perspectives

Listening is a gift we give to one another. The quality of our listening is perhaps the most important factor determining the success of a World Café.

Through practicing shared listening and paying attention to themes, patterns and insights, we begin to sense a connection to a larger whole. Therefore, it is important to encourage people to listen to what is not being spoken along with what is being shared.

7) Share Collective Discoveries

Conversations held at one table reflect a pattern of wholeness that connects with the conversations at the other tables. The last phase of the World Café, often called the "harvest", involves making this pattern of wholeness visible to everyone in a large group conversation.

In order to do that, first invite a few minutes of silent reflection on the patterns, themes and deeper questions experienced in the small group conversations and call them out to share with the larger group.

It is recommended to have a way to capture the harvest – working with a graphic recorder could be useful.

You can visit the *World Café Community Foundation* website to obtain a great deal of resources: *http://www.the-worldcafe.com*

ProAction Café

In October 2014 I had the opportunity to participate in the *Latin American Conference on Agile Methodologies*, held in Medellín, Colombia. On the last day an Open Space took place where the people could propose different sessions and themes (further ahead I'll expand on this kind of dynamic). One of the sessions, proposed by a participant, had as main theme the motivation in self-organized teams and the person who proposed it invited me to be the facilitator of such session, which I accepted.

Twenty minutes later I went to the room selected and the participants started to arrive. It was such a success that the people did not stop coming. At one moment I remember counting about a hundred and twenty people and they kept coming. The challenge I had set myself was to be the facilitator and not the lecturer.

To begin with, I proposed the participants to share their concerns on the subject. A few came up, for example: the motivation in remote teams; in non-hierarchical teams; in teams who perform monotonous activities; in teams under pressure; in recently formed teams, etc.

For each concern, I invited people who had gone through a real experience associated to these topics and we identified them as the *hosts*, then groups of no more than five or six people formed around each host.

Each small group hung a blank poster on the wall and wrote their theme at the top, in big and visible letters that could be repeated together with another group's. Each host talked about their real experience associated to the concern of that group of people.

After that, the participants spent 20 minutes talking with the host and generating ideas that answered the question "which is the real concern behind the experience?" The idea of this conversational cycle was to go beyond the evident.

After those 20 minutes, the people invited rotated to another poster. The host stayed with his/her poster as the owner of the concern.

When a group arrived to the new poster, the host spent 5 minutes bringing them up to date about what had been discussed with the previous group. After that, the new participants spent 20 minutes answering the question "What is missing? What would make this situation more complete? How could the vision of this scenario be expanded?" They presented their answers on post-it notes, which they stuck to the poster.

When those 20 minutes were up, a new rotation took place with the same dynamic as the previous one. After becoming acquainted with the new posters, the groups spent another 20 minutes to answer, together with the host, the following questions: "What have I learned about my concern? What will be my next steps? What help may I still need?" The proposals were written on post-it-notes and then stuck to the posters.

After these last 20 minutes, participants went back to their original posters and spent 10 minutes talking with each host about the findings and answering the questions: "What am I thankful for? What are my next steps?" and recording their answers graphically. At the end, they published their graphics on Twitter with the hashtag *#MotivandoEquipos2014*[10].

---

[10] The translation is #MotivatingTeams2014

This experience I have just explained is the implementation of the *ProAction Café* technique. This technique is a mix of open space and World Café. The dynamic, as a systematic approach, is the following:

1. Each person having a concern, communicate it to the group and choose a table. That person becomes the host of the table.

2. Once all the tables are set, the rest of the people sit at their tables until they complete 4 or 5 people per table.

3. Three 20-minute cycles of conversation take place, answering respectively to the following questions:

    - **Cycle 1:** What is the quest behind the concern?

    - **Cycle 2:** What is missing? How could we complete the scene?

    - **Cycle 3:** What have I learned about my concern? What next steps will I take? What help do I still need?

4. The people invited rotate to other tables between cycles. The host stays at the table.

5. At the end of the three cycles they do an idea-sharing session, where each host tells the whole group:

- What am I thankful for? What learning am I taking with me?
- What am I going to do about it?

Lean Café

In November 2014, almost every member of Kleer met in Medellín. These annual meetings are called *plenaries*.

That time, we decided to make a list of the topics to discuss and a lot of them emerged. It was clear to us that we could not deal with all of them, so, what did we do? We prioritized them, ordered them and discussed one at a time.

Every time we started with a new topic, we set a 10-minute-stopwatch to discuss it. When the time was up, we used the Roman voting method: each person indicated with thumbs up if they wanted to continue with the same subject, the thumbs to one side if it was the same for them of the thumbs down if they wanted to move on to another topic.

If most of the thumbs were up, we continued for another 5 minutes. If only half of the thumbs were up, we continued for another 2 minutes and if the thumbs up were the minority, we moved on to another topic. When the additional time was up, we had a new voting and re-started the cycle. This is called *Lean Café*, which is another technique that can be helpful when it comes to dealing with various subjects.

The possibility to vote at the end of each cycle allows for the group to consciously choose if they want to continue allocating more time to a specific subject, knowing that it is taking time from the other topics.

Tools for Making a Decision

Once the divergent and groan zones were dealt with, and having thought of new possibilities, explored different options, shared perspectives, and analyzed our own way of seeing the world and contrasting it with the rest of the members, it is time to start converging to close the process by making a decision.

To begin the moment of convergence there are several techniques and approaches that can be used. In this next section, I'll present some of them.

Association by Affinity

In many group conversations different ideas emerge which could be grouped by affinity according to the different criteria. The same happens during a *Brainstorming* or *BrainWriting* session.

In these cases, you can resort to association by affinity to group ideas and then prioritize them, order them and vote for them.

The steps to use association by affinity are:

1. Use post-it notes to record the ideas in a visible place such as a *flipchart* or the wall.

2. Invite the participants to group the notes by affinity. This is a process carried out in silence until all the participants have finished.

3. Identify each grouping with a name agreed by the group.

142

4. Once the groups of ideas have been identified, you can continue working with the technique of your preference, it is only necessary to focus on those groupings as a work unit.

Points Based Voting System

I declare myself a fan of *Parking Lots*. In almost all the workshops I facilitate I allocate a specific place to record ideas and questions to discuss and answer later on. Towards the end of the workshop, I usually reserve between 45 to 60 minutes to review all that has been recorded in the *Parking Lot*. This time is not always enough: many times the amount of items is so vast that it is not possible to cover them all.

In these cases, I resort to the **point based voting system**, a very simple and fast mechanism for a group of people to prioritize, in a collaborative way, a series of items in terms of what the group considers more important.

The steps for a point based voting system are the following:

1. Provide each participant with a marker,
2. Invite the participants to distribute three points among the items, in the way they choose:
   - One point for each different item.
   - Two points to an item and one point to another.
   - Three points to only one item.
3. Give some time for the participants to get close to the items and mark their own points.
4. Count the total of points for each item and order them from low to high: the items with the most points are the priority.

As an alternative, the participants may have the possibility to distribute eight points with the condition to only accumulate **up to four points** per item.

Impact Matrix

This is another technique that can help a group of people define priorities. The Impact Matrix has two axes:

- **Axis X**: it represents the effort required to carry out an action and it goes from easy to difficult.

- **Axis Y**: it represents the impact of the action in the defined objective and it goes from low to high impact.

Each possible action is placed in the matrix according to the effort it requires and the impact it will have in the objective posed. This distribution is done after reaching a consensus.

When crossing both axes, four quadrants are formed where the actions are placed:

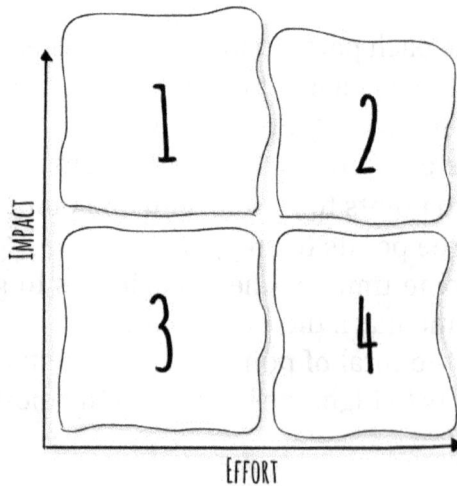

1. **High Impact and Low Effort: priority**. These actions are those called *quick-wins* or *low-hanging-fruit*: things that can be done without much effort and which report a high benefit.

2. **High Impact and High Effort: next priorities**. These are actions which require a higher level of effort but which generate a high benefit.

3. **Low Impact and Low Effort: the third priority**. These are actions that, although they don't report high benefits, they don't involve a high effort either to carry out.

4. **Low Impact and High Effort: actions to discard**. Who wants to invest a great amount of work in actions that don't benefit anyone?

Consensus

Once I had the chance to participate in a homeowner's association meeting where we discussed the problem with a water pump in the building. There were three possible solutions: 1) to install a generator, 2) to connect a new line to the water pump and 3) to buy a second water pump as a back up. There was enough money for only one solution, so we took a vote.

Out of the twelve people present, 5 voted in favor of installing a new generator, four voted in favor of connecting a new line and the rest for a second water pump. The majority decided in favor of option number one.

The second time it was necessary to use the generator, it failed. At that moment, the seven people who had not voted in favor of the solution implemented said: "we warned you".

That is a typical consequence of a decision taken by majority. Every time something that the majority voted for is decided, there is a minority who disagrees. Usually, this is made worse when there are more than two options, because the minorities who lose can add a higher quantity of votes together than the winning option, as was the case in the homeowner's association meeting.

To achieve consensus is very different from majority or unanimous rule. Consensus is reached when the group comes to a sincere agreement, considering and understanding that the option chosen may not be the best from an individual point of view, but it is the best for the group.

It is easier to come to a consensus when each of the members of the group sincerely believes that the rest of the people understand their worries, when they understand each other's concerns, when each person understands everyone else's concerns and, and even when he/she does not prefer the option chosen is willing to support it because they respect the judgment of the group over individual preferences.

At the heart of consensus, there is a conversation among equals based on respect. If the conversation does not happen between equals or one of the members has more hierarchy or more decision power over the rest, a barrier against consensus will be generated.

Absence of equality creates a working context **for** others or **against** others. Nowadays, at organizations, we desperately need to work **with** others. And the road to achieving it is the road to consensus.

Special Section: Open Space

I wanted to discuss Open Space in a special section because I think it is much more comprehensive than the different techniques we have mentioned so far.

We have always organized ourselves to obtain different kinds of goals. Things happen when vision, passion and action are combined, without plans, control or direction.

Prepare to be surprised!

Welcome to Open Space

Open Space is a conversational process created by Harrison Owen. When the author talks about this methodology, he remembers that after having gone through a grueling and laborious year organizing a conference and then having suffered from the stress of coordinating the lecturers, papers, logistics and the participants, he realized that the best moments of the event were the coffee breaks. Why the coffee breaks? Because that's where people get together to talk about what really interests them. Therefore, Owen decided to try a complete conference in coffee break format and that's how Open Space was born.

What is an Open Space?

It is an opportunity to discuss topics that really matter to the participants, without the decisions of an isolated group which risks creating an agenda that does not represent the interests of the majority. The Open Space agenda is created in real-time by the participants of the event.

An Open Space is a conference without a pre-established agenda.

How Does an Open Space Work?

At the beginning the participants sit in a circle or concentric circles. This moment is known as the *Marketplace*.

During the Marketplace, the participants themselves complete a grid with the topics that they are more interested in discussing. This grid contains physical spaces and periods of time, and it represents the calendar for the day. Each topic will be discussed in a specific place and time, according to where it was placed inside the grid.

	ZONE #1	ZONE #2	ZONE #3	ZONE #4	ZONE #5	ZONE N...
10AM – 11AM						
11AM – 12PM						
12PM – 1PM						
1PM – 2PM						
2PM – 3PM						
3PM	CLOSING					

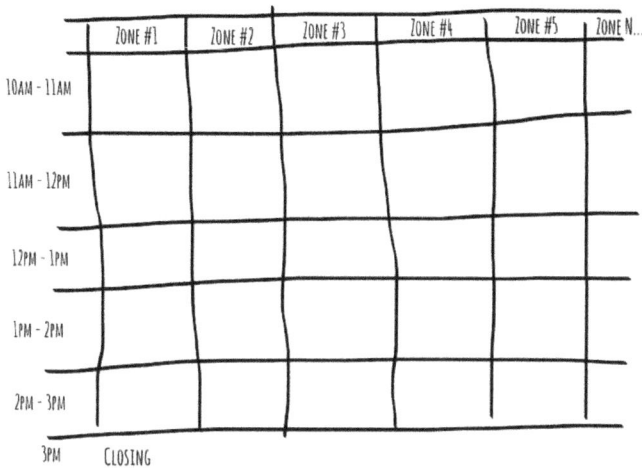

The conversations (also called sessions) take place during most of the day. If new conversations emerge, the people can add them in real time in the calendar of the event, without altering the sessions that have already been scheduled.

At the end of the sessions, the whole group meets to close the event. At that moment, concentric circles begin to form again and the participants share thoughts, comments, perspectives and commitments that have emerged from the conversations.

Four Principles and One Law

An Open Space has only four principles and one law.

The four principles are:

1. Whoever comes is the right people.
2. Whatever happens is the only thing that could have.
3. Whenever it starts is the right time.
4. When it's over, it's over.

149

The law is known as the "The law of two feet":

> *If at any time during our time together you find your-self in any situation where you are neither learning nor contributing, use your two feet and go someplace more productive.*

Food for Thought

Take a few minutes and think about the topic discussed in this chapter.

Below, I share some questions to ask yourself, and answer them if you want to.

1. How consistent were you on decision-making collaborative processes?

2. What have you discovered reading this chapter?

3. What new actions do you think are possible, based on these concepts?

4. During the divergent zone there are factors that can be counterproductive, such as censorship, judgment, criticism. How can you help your team so these factors are not present?

5. In the convergent zone is not recommended to go back to diverge. How do you think you could help your group avoid the divergence?

6. Imagine a group conversation where a lot of divergent ideas arise with no signs of convergence. How do you feel about it?

7. If your answer to the previous question includes a feeling of anxiety, what do you think causes that anxiety?

8. This is the linguistic reconstruction of anxiety (Olalla, 2000)*:*

1. *Something has happened or is happening*
2. *So, something more dangerous can happen*
3. *I don't know how to avoid it*
4. *I can't do anything to change the uncertainty*
5. *I would like to have some certainty*

By reading this linguistic reconstruction, what aspect do you identify in your emotion described in items 6 and 7?

9. What tools from the ones presented in this chapter do you think could help you minimize the uncertainty?

5

KICK-OFF
FACILITATION

In 2002, I was involved in a project to automate a production line and link certain events with a materials management module known as MM to certain events on SAP[11]. The project started like this: my boss at that time handed me a pile of printed sheets of paper as he said, "this is what has to be done, please go over it and let me know if you have any doubts".

I read it and started working on it. As time went by I came across several obstacles of various nature: people who did not get involved, misunderstandings, contradictions with the sheets of papers I had been given, lack of support from customer relationship management and even some people at the client company asked me what was it that we were doing because they were not aware of any projects being carried out... Uhg! In retrospective, I would have given my entire salary for a project kick-off meeting.

---

[11] An integrated ERP system: Enterprise resource planning.

BEGINNING OF AN AGILE PROJECT

The Project kick-off workshop is an activity traditionally known as Project set-up or Project Chartering. Its objectives are:

- To give identity to the project.
- To establish an interpretation base and common agreements.
- To identify the project scope, so it allows the team to make progress with the least amount of friction possible.

In this last six years, I facilitated and assisted in the facilitation of around twenty project kick-off workshops.

Although there are many possible structures for an event of these characteristics, the one that has been more effective to me is a combination of practices and dynamics from different sources.

In this chapter, we will tour an agile project kick-off proposal focusing on the facilitator's role.

ANTICIPATION

As I have already mentioned in previous chapters, the responsibility of the facilitator starts long before the beginning of the meetings or events that are going to be facilitated.

One of the benefits of anticipating is communicating before the meeting the topics that are going to be dealt with, the duration, who will introduce which topic (if it applies), among other aspects.

Anticipating also implies:

- Considering the degree of controversy that the topics to discuss can generate and, in those cases, evaluate the possibility to maintain previous meetings to know the expectations of the participants of the meeting and the scope of their opinions.
- To plan and identify possible dynamics to use in each moment of the meeting.

During the meeting, it is important not to be attached to the designed plan, because what makes anticipating worth it is the activity itself carried out when planning the facilitation. The plan works as a reference that you can come back to in case the process becomes chaotic.

DURATION

The duration of a project kick-off workshop can be from a couple of hours to several days. I have had experiences where the kick-off was complete in two or three hours and experiences where we spent a full five days.

The factors that determine the duration of a project kick-off workshop are:

- The business level of knowledge.
- The expectations of the project scope.
- The amount of people involved.
- The level of clarity about what has to be done and what does not.
- The relationship and experience of the participants working together.

In general, I think a workshop of these characteristics can take two whole days of work. Based on a tentative agenda that contemplates this duration, I meet the interested parties in advance to do the necessary adjustments to then confirm, shorten or lengthen it.

The Tentative Agenda

Below, I'll present a tentative project kick-off agenda. Several of the dynamics mentioned there can be found in *Agile Inception Deck* (Rasmusson, 2010), *User Story Mapping* (Patton & Economy, User Story Mapping: Discover the Whole Story, Build the Right Product, 2014) and in *Impact Mapping* (Adzic, 2012).

Day 1

9:00 AM	Breakfast
9:15 AM	Welcome – What is this?
9:25 AM	Introduction and Work Agreement

10:00 AM	Goal and Vision – Why are we here?
10:45 AM	*Coffee-Break*
11:00 AM	Product/ Service – What are building?
12:00 AM	Community – Who are the *stakeholders* or parties interested in the project?
12:45 PM	Lunch
2:00 PM	Risks – What threats do we foresee?
2:45 PM	Scope – What are going to do and not going to do?
3:45 PM	*Coffee-Break*
4:00 PM	Personas – Who is going to interact?
4:45 PM	Behavior – How do we want to influence people?
5:30 PM	Retrospective of the first day

Día 2

9:00 AM	Breakfast
9:15 AM	Review of the previous day
9:30 AM	*Story Mapping* – What shape is it going to have?
10:45 AM	*Coffee-Break*
11:00 AM	*Story Mapping* - What shape is it going to have? (cont.)

12:00 AM	Sizing – How much work is it?
1:00 PM	Lunch
2:15 PM	Risks – What new threats do we see?
3:45 PM	*Coffee-Break*
4:00 PM	Trade-Off – How flexible is it?
4:45 PM	DoD – What does it mean that something is done?
5:30 PM	Final Retrospective

It is very important to share the agenda in advance with the main interested parties to be able to make adjustments together. Keep in mind that the agenda is only a guide; it is not necessary to strictly enforce it.

The Invitation

The **invitation to the workshop** is as important as the workshop itself. Try to reach the participants with a powerful invitation (McKergow, 2014). This type of invitation recognizes the importance of the participants; it creates attraction and is presented as an option, not as an obligation.

Besides preparing a powerful invitation, I have had very good results when making it personalized, instead of a generic invitation for everyone. Let's analyze two examples.

Weak Invitation:

Hello everyone, I'm sending you this invitation to come to the project kick-off workshop XYZ, which is going to take place in Room 85, next Thursday at 9am.

It will last two days during which we are going to be very focused on working on this new project, that is why I would like to ask you not to use the computers in that period of time.

Looking forward to seeing you!

Powerful Invitation:

Hello Mariano,

I'm writing to invite you to be part of the two-day XYZ project kick-off. Given your experience with the purchase, payment and supplier payment processes, we believe your contribution is key. You are very familiar with purchase order management and the relationship with banks.

We are sure that by involving you from the beginning we will avoid making mistakes and reworking during the project.

We will begin both days at 9 am with breakfast and there will be coffee breaks in the morning and in the afternoon. At noon we will all go to lunch.

We will also experiment with new work dynamics that we are sure you will find very interesting and appealing.

Since we are going to be working with a very specific focus on the project issues, we are inviting everyone to minimize the amount of topics, e-mails and calls during the workshop. Please, let us know if you think we can help you with this requirement.

We assume that your participation is voluntary and, although we do not want you to feel compelled to participate, we are sure your presence will help everyone achieve future objectives, be it the project's, the area's or the company's.

In case you participate, the workshop will take place in Room 85, next Thursday at 9 am.

Please, confirm your presence.

Please let us know if you have any questions.

We look forward to seeing you!

These four elements are present in the second invitation:

1. **Personal**: the name of the recipient appears in the invitation, Mariano.

2. **Recognition**: tells Mariano why his participation is important.

3. **Attraction**: explains some benefits he can obtain by participating in the workshop.

4. **Option**: makes explicit the optional nature of the meeting.

The Participants

The importance of the participants is one of the many differences we find between the Agile Manifesto[12] and the traditional Project managing methodologies.

In Agility, the Project kick-off is considered a collaborative and participative activity. It is the space where relationships start to build and promote debates and agreements.

---

[12] http://www.agilemanifesto.org

The key participants of a project kick-off workshop are the members of the team who will build the product or service, the stakeholders or the people directly interested and the sponsors of the project.

The more diverse the group of people, the better. It is also important for representatives to participate in the business and other areas of the company, such as marketing, product, development, operations, etc.

In my experience, if the amount of people who attend the meeting is more than 10 people, the quality of the participation and the collaboration of the group diminishes. Something you can do to save this situation is to propose that each area involved in the project delegates their participation in a single representative.

If there are participants in the workshop who represent several people in one area, it is vital to create concrete actions that tend to share the outcomes of the meeting as soon as possible, to inform the people represented and obtain their feedback quickly.

PUNCTUALITY

In my opinion, punctuality is important.

I think people who are late are disrespectful and careless towards others: it confuses, disorganizes, promotes distrust, obstructs. How many times has it happened to you that it is necessary to repeat what you have already said because someone didn't arrive at the time agreed? How many times have you been involved in conversations about decisions that had already been taken, but in which certain people were not present?

I prefer to avoid these situations as much as possible. Therefore, I always arrange for participants to arrive 15 minutes before the beginning of the activity and to have snacks and refreshments for the participants to get some breakfast before starting. This increases the amount of attendees at the beginning of activities and avoids significant delays. An alternative I tried and worked very well was to use non-conventional schedules as surprise elements to capture the participants' attention, for example:

8:57 AM	Breakfast
9:18 AM	Welcome – What is this?
9:32 AM	Introduction – Who is who?
10:06 AM	Objective and Vision – Why are we here?
10:51 AM	*Coffee-Break*

Facilitation of dynamics

In this section, I'll briefly show you the activities I usually use for each moment of the agenda in a project kick-off workshop.

Welcome – What is This?

We have already established the importance of communicating the objective of the meetings we facilitate: it is ideal that all the participants have a clear reason why they attend this workshop. For this reason, it is good to remember the goal during the welcome. And, although this moment of the agenda is important so is to be brief and concise.

A good dynamic to establish the connection between the participants and the purpose of the project kick-off workshop is the following:

1. Invite the participants to form pairs; if they are an odd number, there will be a triad.

2. Ask the small groups to remember, in 5 minutes, significant problems they have had in the execution of previous projects. What could have they done at the beginning of these projects to avoid problems or minimize them?

3. Give each pair a 5 to 10 minute timebox to share their answers to the previous questions with the rest of the participants.

After this dynamic, explicitly share the purpose of the Project kick-off workshop with the rest of the participants.

Introduction and Work Agreement

This is a good time for participants to introduce themselves based on some dynamic. You can invite them to introduce themselves in pairs and then members introduce their partner to the rest of the group.

In general, I don't do anything very sophisticated since the participants are going to be working together and getting to know each other during the workshop.

At this moment, it is also important to establish the contract or work agreement for this workshop. This is a challenge that the participants can solve themselves. Usually, I ask them to write a list of things they would like to happen and things they would like to avoid during the workshop. This helps maximize the participation, collaboration and mutual respect.

Reminding the participants of this agreement during the workshop is not something I enjoy. Therefore, I put the agreement in one or two posters on the walls so it is clearly visible to everyone. The participants themselves can use these posters as a reference during the workshop.

Objective and Vision – Why are We Here?

The goal of this part of the workshop is to present the objective posed as well as the vision of this project.

In 1998, I had the opportunity to work in a technology project. It was the migration of around 900 input and output data interfaces to an IBM AS/400 system. When I started, they gave us the schedule and the technical details of the interfaces developed in a language called *Delphi*, which we had to migrate to another language called *C++*.

Finding motivations and taking decisions in this Project was very difficult. For example, I never knew the reason why we had to do this job. Knowing the business need that generated this effort would have helped a lot.

Many work teams have trouble getting organized since they lack visibility and conscience on the impact of their decisions. To avoid this situation it is important for the participants to know the *why* (Rasmusson, 2010) of what they are doing. This link between the tasks they have to do and its business goal helps any self-organized context when making intrinsic decisions.

Unlike traditional methodologies that consider that project is successful when it is delivered in time, manner and according to scope, Agile Methodologies also consider that if a product or project achieved its expected business objectives, then it is successful from a business point of view, even if the scope is different to the one specified initially. In fact, if the project is delivered respecting the exact predefined scope but does not comply with the business objective, it is considered a failure (Adzic, 2012).

As much as it is important to know one or several business goals, it is even more important to measure the achievement of those goals. Therefore, it is necessary for the facilitator to anticipate and know –before the workshop- the business objectives and promote their S.M.A.R.T. characteristics (Doran, 1981): [S]pecific, [M]easurable, [A]chievable, [R]elevant and [T]ime-bound.

For example, "I want to lose weight" is an objective that does not comply with these characteristics. There are a series of questions that can be asked to help the interested party turn that wish into a SMART objective:

1. How much weight do you want to lose? *16 lbs.* (makes it measurable).

171

2. How long would it take you to lose that amount of weight? *2 months* (has an established time frame).
3. This would involve losing 2 lbs. per week; do you think you can do it? *No* (then, it is not realistic or assignable).
4. And how much are you willing to lose per week? *1lb.* (It is realistic and assignable).
5. So, that means that you would lose 16 lbs. in four months (16 weeks). *Correct.*

Therefore, the redefined objective is to "Lose 16 lbs. in four months".

IT IS IMPORTANT TO HELP THE PRODUCT OWNER SO THAT THE BUSINESS OBJECTIVES PRESENTED TO THE TEAM ARE S.M.A.R.T.

At this stage of the workshop we also explain the vision, that future scenario desired when building this product or service. There are different strategies to establish a vision that depend on the level of participation there is in the organization and the learning capacity of its members (Senge, 2012). These strategies can be:

- **Telling**: the leader communicates the vision and the team must follow it.
- **Selling**: the leader knows the vision and communicates it in a way that the team "buys" it to move forward.

- **Testing**: the leader has a clear idea about which should be the vision and communicates it to know the reactions of the team before advancing with the project.
- **Consulting**: the leader has a vision in progress and needs the assistance of part of the team to be able to continue.
- **Co-creating**: leader and team, through collaborative exercises, they build together a shared vision.

"IT IS AN IMPORTANT DAY IN EVERYONE'S LIFE WHEN THEY BEGIN TO WORK FOR WHAT THEY WANT TO BUILD RATHER THAN TO PLEASE A BOSS."
PETER SENGE, QUOTING BILL O'BRIEN

What we are interested in as facilitators is to achieve a shared and co-created vision by the team and the stakeholders, or interested parties. A vision that appeals to the involvement and creativity of the people. In order to do that, I have successfully used a dynamic called Remember the Future (Hohmann , 2006), explained below:

1. Hand each participant a sheet of paper.

2. Invite the group to go on a mental trip in time to a future date where they imagine themselves using the product or service in question for a week, month or a quarter.

3. Then, suggest that they go further ahead in the future, for example a week, two weeks, or a month after the previous testing period.

4. Ask them to write in the blank sheet of paper what the product or service has done for them and thanks to which they consider themselves happy (secure, or rich or successful or whatever may work).

5. Facilitate a sharing session of what was recorded and agree on the shared vision.

Another alternative is that the group writes the front page of a newspaper with a piece of news referring to the benefits of the product or service already developed.

Having said that, many times it is not possible to build a shared vision. In that case, you will have to resort to some of the other strategies proposed by Senge: consulting, testing, selling or telling.

The important thing is to leave the door open to a road that will lead the team and eventually the organization to the creation of future shared visions.

DAILY RETROSPECTIVES

If there is anything significant I learned from experience these last years is the importance of doing a small retrospective to close all the meetings. It is something that takes little time and which gives you the possibility of obtaining real time *feedback* on your facilitation.

You can use different dynamics at his moment, according to the time available and the amount of participants in the meeting. Below, I'll present some examples.

Keep, Fix, Try (15 to 30 minutes)

It is a classic dynamic that can be used to listen to the participants' impression:

1. A table with three columns is generated in a poster or on the wall with the words 'Keep, 'Fix' and 'Try'.

2. Then, invite the participants to think for 5 minutes about those aspects of the meeting that they would like to keep, fix and try in future editions and write these aspects on different post-it notes.

3. Finally, the retrospective closes with the participants sharing their thoughts while they stick their post-it notes in the different columns.

Dynamic, logistics, content, participants (10 to 15 minutes)

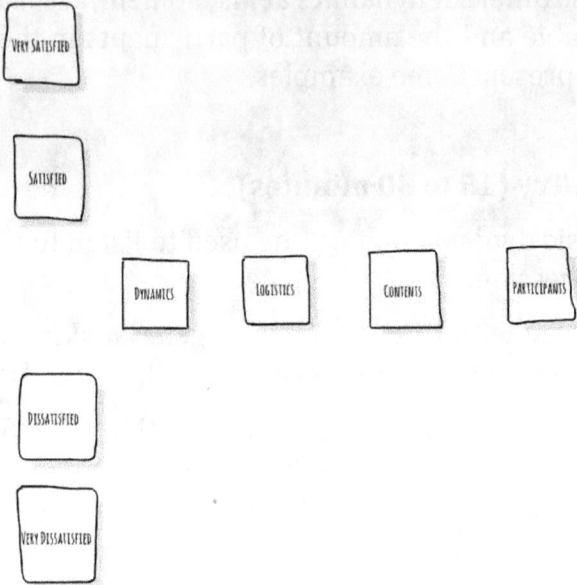

This activity takes less time than the previous one and the focus is on those changes that the participants consider necessary:

1. **Categories**: on the same line put 4 post-it notes on the wall or on a poster board with the headings:

   - Dynamics

   - Logistics

   - Content

   - Participants

2. **Level of satisfaction:** to the left of the category row, put a column with four post-it notes, two above the category row and two under it. The figure would be similar to a T leaning to the left.

   The post-it notes of the column indicate the following:

   - Very satisfied

   - Satisfied

   - Dissatisfied

   - Very dissatisfied

3. Each participant is invited to express their level of satisfaction on each category, sticking their post-it notes in the corresponding height.

4. As the participants stick their notes they can explain their impressions aloud.

An alternative is to invite the participants to write a suggestion on each note they stick in the categories where they are dissatisfied or very dissatisfied.

Return On Time Invested [ROTI] (5 to 10 minutes)

This activity allows you to quickly measure the level of overall satisfaction in regards to the meeting and the time invested

(Larsen & Derby, 2006). Since it is an activity created for situations where time is very limited, it does not go too deep into the participants' feedback. To use it you can follow the next steps:

1. Represent a vertical scale from 1 to 4 drawn on a poster or using sticky notes on the wall. Each number of the scale represents the satisfaction regarding the time invested:

   - **Excellent**: a very useful meeting whose value exceeded by far the time invested.

   - **Above average**: a meeting that produced a value that exceeded the time invested.

   - **Below Average**: The value received was not enough compared with the time invested.

   - **Useless**: I didn't receive any value at all.

2. Ask the participants to specify their level of satisfaction regarding the time invested.

An alternative to this activity in situations where there is more time is to add 5 to 10 additional minutes to look into the participants' ratings, especially those in the lowest scale.

Net Promoter Score [NPS] (less than 5 minutes)

The *Net Promoter*[13] business indicator represents the satisfaction that an organization provides to its clients. You can use this same technique to quickly measure the satisfaction of the participants in the meeting. It is a very fast technique, without looking into or going deep into the details, it can give you a good idea on the level of satisfaction. The steps to follow when implementing it are:

1. Invite the participants to think about and hand out a piece of paper with a number from 0 to 10 which represents their personal answers to the question: Would you recommend this meeting to a colleague or friend? 10 representing *definitely yes* and 0, *definitely not.*

2. Gather all the answers after you close the meeting.

3. Identify those answers with 9 and 10. This is the amount of promoting participants. Calculate the percentage of the total of participants who represent the promoters.

4. Identify those answers from between 0 and 6. This is the number of detractors. Calculate the total percentage of participants who represent the detractors.

5. Dismiss answers with 7 and 8.

6. The *NPS* of a meeting is the percentage of promoters minus the percentage of detractors. A number close to 100 represents the highest satisfaction while a number close to -100 represents a high dissatisfaction.

Remember that this technique is useful to identify the level of satisfaction fast and without going deep into details. If what you are looking for is indeed to improve the experience, you

---

[13]https://www.netpromoter.com

will have to look into the aspects that can be improved. That will take you longer, and if you have the time, I recommend you to privilege some of the previously presented techniques.

Review of the Previous Day

A very healthy way to begin a second day is refreshing the concepts discussed and the decisions taken on the day before. A dynamic that has given me good results is the one called Gallery Walk.

If the activities of the previous day created posters, drawings, lists, sticky notes, and they remain stuck to the walls, you can invite the participants to form groups of two or three people to walk around the room, contemplate each of the posters for a few minutes and discuss what they remember doing on the previous day.

The time the walk takes can span 5 to 10 minutes. After that, we suggest you have a sharing session to go over the different topics discussed with all the participants.

This activity generates connections with the topics discussed on the first day and predisposes the participants to start the meeting agenda of the new day in a more informed manner.

The Other Dynamics of the Workshop

The remaining dynamics which conform the project kick-off workshop are described in detail in Agile Samurai (Rasmusson, 2010), User Story Mapping (Patton & Economy, User Story Mapping: Discover the Whole Story, Build the Right Product, 2014), Impact Mapping (Adzic, 2012) and Agile Projects with Scrum (Alaimo & Salias, Proyectos Ágiles con Scrum: Flexibilidad, aprendizaje, innovación y colaboración en contextos complejos, 2015).

In any case, below I share a very brief description of each one and leave references so you can go deeper into them.

Product/Service: What are we going to build?

The goal here is to achieve clarity on what the team needs to build and that the participants of the workshop get close to the consumers or end users of the product or service.

Two activities that can be useful in this case, as proposed in a Project Inception meeting (Rasmusson, 2010), are the creation of an Elevator Pitch of the Product (Moore, 2006) and a Vision Box (Hohmann , 2006).

Community: Who are the Stakeholders?

This exercise proposes that all the participants of the workshop identify the interested parties.

Identifying the stakeholders, understanding their degree of influence in a project and the balance of their demands, needs and expectations are critical aspects for the success of the project. If this does not happen, there could be future delays, increase in costs, unexpected problems and other negative consequences, including the cancellation of the project (PMI, 2013).

Scope: What are we going to do and not?

It is as important to agree on what the team will build as it is agreeing on what the team is not going to build.

For that, you can organize the participants in different teams in charge of identifying what will be done, what will not be done and what things are not possible to decide if they will be done or not (Alaimo & Salias, 2015).

Personas: Who is going to interact?

To define what is valuable and what is not, it is vital to identify the people we intend to add value through the solution that we are going to build. A very simple technique, taken from the marketing area, is the People Meter (Nielsen).

It consists of identifying different segments of clients of our product or service through the creation of a fictional character with a name, photograph and typical characteristics of that segment.

Behavior: How do we want to influence?

This activity focuses on identifying the changes you want to generate in the behavior of the people through our product or service. What do we want them to do? (Ulwick, 2005)

Story Mapping: What shape is it going to have?

A User Story Map will organize the characteristics of the product or service in a useful model to understand the priorities and establish a delivery strategy that offers value to the clients in each delivery (Patton, 2008).

Briefly, it is about identifying the different activities that a person has to do to comply with a business process and it determines an evolutionary strategy of product building, so that the necessary support can be provided to each of these activities in an evolutionary way.

Sizing: How much work is necessary?

Once the characteristics of the product or service have been identified we proceed to estimate the amount of work required to build it and implement it. Two techniques that are commonly used in these cases are Planning Poker (Cohn, 2005) and Team Estimation.

Risks: What threats do we foresee?

There are many dynamics that can be used to identify risks. In general, they are classified according to the probability of its occurrence and impact. I like to draw a bi-dimensional matrix on a poster and represent the risks using post-it notes, placed in the agreed coordinates. After identifying the 5 or 10 most important risks, the participants can work in teams to create contingency plans, mitigation or outsourcing.

Trade-Off: How much flexibility is there?

All the projects have parameters that can be equalized in time, money, scope and quality. The ideal is to know what factor is more important and how flexible each of them is (Rasmusson, 2010). A very interesting dynamic can be The Equalizer, an activity that I discussed in previous pages. In order to use this technique, you need to form an equalizer on the floor and mark the equilibrium points for each parameter, with the same people standing in the place that represents the corresponding level of flexibility (Alaimo & Salias, 2015).

DoD: What does it mean that something is done?

DoD stands for Definition of Done. As much as it is important to know how much time the construction is required and what is expected of certain product or service features, it is also important to have a quality agreement that can be useful to identify and make explicit the expectations implying that something is done. For that, you can organize the people in small groups to talk for a few minutes about their expectations on completing deliverables. Afterwards, you can facilitate a sharing session where formal or informal agreements are generated among the members to avoid future misunderstandings.

So far, we have discussed different techniques for the facilitation of a project kick-off workshop. In the next chapter we'll discuss other techniques, recommendations and experiences in the facilitation of meetings that take place during an agile iteration.

6

SPRINT
FACILITATION

In this chapter, I will focus on the facilitation of a team working under the Scrum framework. As I have mentioned at the beginning of this book, I will assume you know what agility and Scrum are. In case you don't, I recommend you to read more about them on https://chiefagilityofficer.com

Sprint Planning

A sprint planning meeting involves answering the following questions (Schwaber & Sutherland, Scrum Guide, 2013):

1. What can be delivered in the increment resulting from the upcoming sprint?
2. How will the work needed to deliver the increment be achieved?

As a facilitator, the objectives to follow so the team and the stakeholders can answer these questions are:

- That the expectations of the stakeholders are known and explicit in regards to the features expected for the product or service.
- That the team generates the necessary commitment to building a product or service increment and deliver it at the end of the sprint.
- That the team coordinates the appropriate actions among its members to create a high-level plan with the tasks for the sprint backlog.

At the end of the planning meeting, the team should have added two new elements:

1. A goal for the new sprint.
2. A list of features for the product or service increment, and the tasks related to it: the sprint backlog.

ANTICIPATION

As we have seen throughout the book, an important component in the work of every facilitator is anticipation. In the case of the sprint planning meeting, the anticipation is focused on the product backlog, its items, and participants.

DEEP BACKLOG

In this case, it is important to work constantly with the product owner and help him maintain the product backlog so that it's DEEP (Pichler, 2010):

- **Detailed appropriately**: a product backlog should have an appropriate level of detail in the high priority items and progressively reduce its level of detail as the priority of the items decreases. In a sprint planning meeting, the items with the highest priority are the ones that concern us the most. It is important to keep them detailed enough so that the members of the team feel safe to take the commitment for the sprint.

- **Estimated**: part of the sprint planning meeting includes estimating the items. In my experience, the teams achieve better results when the items in the product backlog have been estimated ahead of this meeting. This estimation can take place during the sprint or in a meeting dedicated to refining the product backlog. Later, the estimation is confirmed during the planning meeting.

- **Emergent**: the product backlog is not a static element: it is alive, organic, it grows. This variability is given by the feedback and stakeholders' learning process that the team acquires in time. Before planning the new sprint, it is key to work along with the product owner to help him include all the feedback and the learning process of the previous sprint in the product backlog.

- **Prioritized**: a healthy product backlog represents the creation strategy of the product or service by means of prioritizing its items. Before a sprint meeting, it is important that the product owner has the priority of each item identified. A recommendation would be that the product owner comes to the sprint planning meeting prepared to talk about two sprint's worth of product backlog items (Cohn).

READY

A usual practice to optimize the use of time during the sprint planning meeting is to take the items of the product backlog ready enough for the members of the team to assume the commitment to finishing them on that sprint. "Ready enough" is an agreement to be generated within the team and is commonly known as Definition of Ready (DoR). Regarding this aspect, Jeff Sutherland recommends the following model to define an item of the product backlog (Sutherland, Definition Of Ready, 2014):

1. It has to be defined with enough clarity so that all the members of the team understand what needs to be done.
2. It includes a clear definition of the value that it provides to the business so that the product owner can understand its priority.
3. It includes any other feature that increases its clarity: specifications, sketches, wire-frames, etc.
4. It fully satisfies the criteria of INVEST.
5. It is free of external dependences.

The mnemonic rule INVEST (Wake, 2003) is a good guide to foster product backlog items that are granular and understandable to everyone:

- I: independent,
- N: negotiable,
- V: valuable for the clients,
- E: estimable,
- S: small and
- T: testable.

Participants

A discussion I usually see myself involved in revolves around the participants of a planning meeting.

By definition, all the team participates in a meeting of this type: the product owner, the construction team and the facilitator (Schwaber & Sutherland, Scrum Guide, 2013).

Stakeholders

The previous definition of sprint planning does not mention the participation of the stakeholders or interested parties. In my personal experience, the best results were obtained when the key stakeholders participated, those people linked to the items of the product backlog which could be committed in the new sprint.

From my point of view, their participation is essential, and many times I also encourage the participation of the project sponsor. I have observed how the collaboration and the feeling of the team emerge thanks to the interaction between the interested parties and the team. My feeling is that a new team emerges, of a higher level, where transparency, visibility and the knowledge of the business are encouraged.

Part-timers

One of the fundamental pillars of agility is *focus*. When people can focus on their work, it significantly contributes to quality and creativity. That is why it is recommended to work on one project at a time.

Now, achieving that level of focus, often takes a considerable amount of time, and it is part of an organizational transformation that involves structural as well as cultural issues. In many organizations, working on a single project tends to be a utopic scenario due to the high specialization of the people.

For these reasons, as long as the background objective is preserved –which is to lower the level of specialization and achieving multidisciplinary profiles-, as they participate in a process of transformation, we will have to learn to live with part-time team members. These members can be designers, experts in usability, architects, security specialists, etc. They all share a fundamental characteristic: they provide a service to several teams in parallel.

If there are people with this characteristic in the team you facilitate, remember to invite them to the sprint planning meeting. Something that usually happens in these kind of scenarios is to leave these people out of the planning and assume commitments in their name, which does not always lead to good results.

Structure and Dynamic

Once the sprint planning meeting has started, the focus of the facilitation is concentrated on the process. In this case, a little facilitation is required, even at the beginning. To offer teams a structure that can be used to plan the sprint is enough for them to go ahead with it on their own (Adkins, 2010).

Below, I detail some aspects to consider, all related to the structure and dynamics of the sprint planning meeting.

Agenda

An agenda that is visible to everyone helps the meeting to flow and avoid diversions, and unnecessary ramifications. If any possible distraction appears, you just need to remind the participants of the primary objective of this meeting: to plan the sprint.

Stopwatch

"We don't have enough time." It is very typical to hear this statement with which I disagree.

Time is time; no one has more or less time than another person. Therefore, it is impossible for time to run out. They key is *how* we administer our time. And in general, myself included, we do it very poorly due to a lack of awareness. For example, we don't know how much time has passed or how long we have left. Hence, using a visible stopwatch and establishing a time-box[14]

---

[14] Time-boxing is a time management technique which consists of defining a limited amount of time to carry out a task or deal with an issue.

is key during these kind of meetings, since it helps the participants to self-manage their time.

It is likely that at the beginning it is necessary to show them the stopwatch to remind the participants of the amount of time available. As the team develops their own experience in these meetings, the facilitator will be able to gradually step away to let the participants manage time on their own.

Parking-Lot

My recommendation is that you arrange a parking lot for emerging actions. Many times doubts come up as well as information needs or tests to be done. If not recorded somewhere, there is risk for them of getting lost on the way. A parking-lot where you can place sticky notes with emerging topics will help not losing sight of them. My recommendation is that each item has a clear person responsible for it.

Sprint Goal

One of the first activities I recommend facilitating during a sprint planning meeting is to establish the goal for the new sprint.

> If you don't know where you are going, any road will take you there. Lewis Carroll

The sprint would have a shared goal so it help all team members to move in the same direction. Once the objective has been established, the members of the team are responsible for achieving it (Pichler, 2010).

To have a clear goal for the sprint is vital for the team to be able to make decisions autonomously during the execution, such as: to change a priority, redefining a feature, negotiate a scope cut and, even, to propose the cancelation of a sprint. All these decisions will better respond to the emerging problem if they are made with full knowledge of the objective of the sprint.

I recommend helping the stakeholders and the product owner to relate the sprint goal with the business objectives. So, the work begins to show certain explicit coherence.

What Are We Going to Do?

Once the sprint goal has been established, it is time to determine the product or service increment that will be delivered at the end of the cycle. In this instance, the prioritized product backlog should be available with the detailed items that are the candidates for this sprint, so that the team can make their commitments.

An element that works very well to contextualize and maintain focused conversations is a panel of activities with three columns. The first column corresponds to the pending, and it is where the items of the product backlog are placed. When one of the items is discussed, it is moved to the second column known as 'in progress' and, once finished, it goes to the third column of finished items. This happens one item at a time, while the team assumes their commitments for the sprint.

This activity finishes when the team determines that they cannot commit to assuming more work for the new sprint.

Respect the Commitment of the Team

One of the most frequent problems, and I dares ay that it is inherited from more authoritarian models, is the pressure exerted to the team so they do the most amount of work in the least amount of time. This behavior can be observed when the product owner questions the work limit decided by the team, the way in which they do things or when they try to minimize the amount of work needed to be done. Under extreme situations, it is possible to observe the product owner asking the members of the team to work overtime.

As a facilitator, it is important to be aware of these situations and evidence them. Agility promotes a sustainable pace indefinitely, and that implies minimizing overtime.

How Are We Going to Do It?

Once all the items committed to the sprint have been identified, it is time to determine the tasks that should be done to deliver the product or service increment and, eventually a high-level technical design or agreement.

In this part of the meeting, the usual is that only the facilitator remains working with the team, whereas the stakeholders leave.

Some teams choose to include the product owner during this activity; other teams prefer not to force him/her to participate. Whatever the case may be, it is important to make sure that the decision is made conscientiously and not because it says so in a book.

If the product owner participates in this part of the meeting, you will have to be alert that he/she does not exert any influence on the way the team performs the tasks, which is the exclusive right of the rest of the team.

A Day or Less

During this part of the meeting, the facilitator can help the team so that all the tasks are granular enough, so they take a day or even less.

One of the original recommendations was that the tasks took approximately between 4 to 16 hours (Schwaber & Beedle , 2001). The idea behind this recommendation is based on the balance between visibility and administrative overload: if the tasks are very granular, the effort to manage them is too much; if they are too big, it is difficult to visualize the progress.

Nowadays, there is a school of thought and action which fosters a decomposition of the tasks until they take a day or less. If the tasks are dimensioned so that no one takes more than a day and if the team meets every day to synchronize, when the same task is in progress for two consecutive days it is a possible sign of delay, since it is taking more than a day to be finished.

For this segment of the planning meeting, it is usually recommended to use two facilitation dynamics: mind mapping and silent tasking (Adkins, 2010). My suggestion is that the team can experience and find the best option for themselves. There will always be a retrospective at the end of the road to inspect and adapt.

High-level Design

During the search for tasks and planning of the sprint arises the need to design what will be done. The important thing at this point is that the design focuses exclusively on the new sprint and does not extend beyond what they have committed to. Every design at this point is an agreement and not a rigid commitment. If the result of this design conversation needs changes during the execution of the sprint, it is important that these changes are visible to the rest of the team.

Planning Retrospective

As usual, at the end of the meeting, I recommend doing a quick retrospective to provide information to improve the dynamics of the meeting, the agenda, the logistics, etc. You can use some of the dynamics previously mentioned in chapter 6.

Daily meeting

The objective desired through the daily meetings is to promote the communication and transparency within the team, which facilitates the coordination of actions between its members and the knowledge of the dependency levels of the activities performed.

In these meetings, the commitments assumed among the members of the team are also strengthened and the obstacles that arise from the work being carried out, which many times obstruct the achievement of the objectives posed are explicit (Alaimo, 2013).

The mechanism to advance in these meetings is very simple: the members of the team meet every day for no more than 15 minutes. Each of the members answers three questions aloud:

1. What did I do since the last daily meeting until now?

2. What am I going to do before the next daily meeting?

3. What are the obstacles that don't let me move forward?

Commitments and Responsibility

> *The commitments have two sides: for a commitment to exist there has to be at least someone who commits and someone who receives (or does not) the object of the commitment.*
>
> *Requests, as well as offers, are seeds for the generation of agreements among the people. When I offer something, and you accept it, then there is a commit-*

> *ment from me to you. Conversely, when I ask some-*
> *thing from you, and you accept it, then there is a com-*
> *mitment from you to me.*
>
> *(Alaimo, 2013)*

Every time a member of the team explains what he/she is going to do before the next daily meeting, he/she assumes a new commitment. Therefore, day after day, the members of the team assume their commitments with the rest of the team present.

> *Healthy agile teams experience peer pressure. In*
> *these teams, all the members have committed to fin-*
> *ishing certain tasks together. This makes the work*
> *and the people independent and responsible to each*
> *other (Adkins, 2010).*

When a member of the team explains what he/she did between a meeting and the next, what is expected is that it matches what he/she said was going to do. If it doesn't happen, then there is a certain contradiction with the commitments assumed. If during several consecutive days a member of the team does not do what he/she said, it is taken as a sign of alarm which will have to be communicated and solved by the team itself. The role of facilitator, at this moment, is to be the catalyzer but never the controller.

Visibility

In 1995, I took one of my first steps in web development. It was something very incipient, entirely new. A TV channel hired us to publish their program grid on their website. A short while after beginning the project, I remember spending a whole night learning to draw on a website the program grid which was read from a database.

When the next day I arrived at the office very excited for my achievement, I found out that another of my workmates had also stayed up solving the same problem.

Has it ever happened to you that you are working on the same project as your desktop neighbor but you have no idea what he is working on? And has it ever happened to you that you face a problem that somebody else already solved but as you don't know that, you spend time trying to solve in it your way? And that someone approaches a problem you have already solved, and neither of you find out about it until it is too late?

Well, these are the situations that a daily meeting intends to solve through visibility.

Meeting just 15 minutes or less, if possible, every day, helps make the commitments, the obstacles, and the work shared, visible. In this way, the team works in a synchronized way, re-work risks are minimized and at the same time, the possibilities of collaboration are maximized.

Inspect and Adapt

The possibility of inspection and adaptation in short periods of time is what allows agile teams to react to changes in the context and unexpected situations quickly while the cost and the impact are still small.

Agile teams use these periods of inspection and adaptation on various levels and instances of the work process. One of these instances is, precisely, daily meetings.

Reviewing the context –what we did, what we are doing, what we are going to do, what are the obstacles- periodically and frequently, allows an agile team to re-plan their work in real time and, therefore, adapt on a daily basis to the reigning circumstances.

Focus and Time-boxing

During the daily meeting, the facilitator should help the team members focusing on the issues that correspond to such meeting. Some signs that the focus is elsewhere are: the conversations in parallel; more than one person speaking at the same time; conversations about topics that are not related to the work being done; the attempt to solve problems during the meeting, etc.

An efficient technique to promote the focus and time-boxing during the meeting is the use of the token, a random element such as an anti-stress ball, a marker, the post-it pad, a notepad, etc. the token is passed from person to person and only that person who has it can speak. When that person finishes, he/she passes the token to the next person and so on.

As we have discussed in previous pages, a visible stopwatch also helps the members of an agile team to manage efficiently the time available and encourages members to come to the daily meetings prepared, instead of improvising, when it is time to speak.

To hold the daily meeting in front of the task board helps maintain the focus and promotes visibility based on the movement of the sticky notes as they speak. It also contributes to strengthening the commitment and gives them satisfaction when they see a new finished task.

Removing Obstacles

All the obstacles that arise from the daily meeting turn into the facilitator's responsibility: it is important to solve them as soon as possible[15].

Except the technical obstacles –which the members of the team are directly responsible for-, the facilitator leaves the daily meeting with the impediments to be solved.

A very useful way for the teams to visualize the progress of obstacle removal is to have an obstacle board. To this effect, you can use the task board, presented in previous chapters, which many teams use to have a visual of the work during the sprint.

In this sense, I think that the facilitator has to participate actively towards the end of the daily meeting answering the following questions:

---

[15] Personally, I think that the facilitator should evolve to a coaching role where he/she is not directly but indirectly responsible of the obstacle removal. I will go deeper into this subject in *agile team coach*, the second book of this collection of books. For now, it is assumed that the facilitator is directly responsible for the resolution of the obstacles.

- What obstacles did I work on since the last daily meeting?
- What obstacles am I going to work on before the next daily meeting?
- What are the obstacles I'm having trouble progressing with and why?

What a Daily Meeting is not

In many cases, a daily meeting is confused with another kind of meeting, due to a lack of knowledge or to attachment to the past. Next, I'll present a series of meetings a daily meeting can turn into if you are not alert to it.

A Status Report

I think a daily meeting has transformed into a status report when I see that all the members of the team talk to only one person: the facilitator. Everyone gathers and look at the facilitator as they tell him/her what they did, what they will do and the obstacles that don't let them move forward.

These kind of daily meetings do not promote the conversation or synchronization among the members of the team. It is only useful for the facilitator to know what each of them has been working on. This issue gets worse when the facilitator takes note of what each person says so that "there is some evidence". From my point of view, this behavior is a clear signal of context where trust is lacking.

Another aggravating situation happens when during the daily meeting the facilitator or a person external to the team asks for explanations about the reasons why they are doing such and such a thing.

Recommendations for the facilitator:

- To avoid making eye contact with the person who is speaking. Doing so will invite him/her to make eye contact with other members of the team.
- Place yourself outside the circle formed by the participants. In this way, the facilitator stays out of the line of sight and reinforces the nature of this meeting: from the team to the team.
- Avoid taking notes. If you need to leave evidence of what was discussed, let the task board be the main support.
- Don't poke your fingers into other people's pie. Avoid the intervention of people external to the team. For this purpose, you can have meetings with these people before they participate as listeners, making special emphasis on what is and is not expected of them.

An Opportunity to Change the Scope of the Sprint

The scope of the sprint is the work that the team committed to doing in the planning meeting. In many cases, especially when a team is new in the use of Agile Methodologies, an attempt is made to change the scope during its execution. Scope changes during the sprint is something that the facilitator has to avoid. The scope agreed is maintained during the entire sprint, and it should not be altered.

The change of scope during the sprint is a symptom of a lack of clarity in the product vision, of an absence of the sprint objective or of product backlog priorities that have not been established.

The most commonly used way to try to introduce changes to the scope during a sprint is, precisely, the daily meeting. Something similar to this usually happens: at the beginning of the meeting the facilitator talks about a new feature that needs to be added in that sprint and asks: what features of the already committed ones could be removed to be able to include this one? Many times the members of the team want to know more about such modification to be able to estimate the required work for it. And so, 15 minutes of the daily meeting end up being used for something else.

Recommendations for the facilitator:

- Raise awareness that the team should not use uses more than 15 minutes to achieve the objective of the daily meeting: synchronize as a team.
- Promote the avoidance of scope changes during a sprint.
- If the change of scope is inevitable, call for a meeting between the team and the product owner to evaluate the cancellation of the current sprint and the beginning of a new one.
- If these situations repeat, help the product owner establish the priorities and to generate agreements with the stakeholders.
- If these situations keep happening, evaluate the current duration of the sprints, it may need to be shorter. The rule of thumb is: the higher the uncertainty and volatility, the shorter the sprints.

A Technical Discussion

Technical discussions tend to be one of the most common problems why the 15 minutes of the daily meeting cannot be used efficiently.

Not long ago I attended a daily meeting that a team of five people were having. When it was his/her turn, one of them made a comment about a technical obstacle and another person asked questions to know more about the situation. A few seconds later, that conversation had turned into a constructive discussion about how to solve such obstacle. After a few minutes, the rest of the members of the team were looking at the ceiling while the other two kept talking about the best technical solution for that problem. Very few daily meetings of this nature are necessary for the people who are out of these conversations to start consider them a waste of time.

Recommendations for the facilitator:

- Help team members maintain only one conversation going on during the daily meeting. If different conversations emerge in parallel, ask for silence, remind them of the objective and invite them to continue with only one conversation.
- If new technical obstacles appear and someone manifests their intention to cooperate in the solution or wants to know more about the problem, suggest the members of the people involved to have that conversation outside the space assigned to the daily meeting. For example, they can talk about it when the meeting finishes or whenever they agree to do it.

AN OPPORTUNITY FOR COMMAND AND CONTROL

- What happened with what you said yesterday that you were going to do?
- Have you been able to solve that obstacle?
- Why are you going to start doing that?
- Why don't you do this other thing?
- Today you should start with this task.

All these are questions and expressions that the facilitator could say and, without realizing it, transform the daily meeting into a command and control meeting.

It is important to remember that the goal of this meeting is that the team synchronizes. The ideal would be that these type of questions, complaints and suggestions were done by the members of the team themselves (peer pressure) outside the daily meeting.

RESISTING BOREDOM

Do not be alarmed if after a few months of daily meetings, they become boring. Many times it happens because they become monotonous and predictable, and the members of the team stop considering it valuable. Next, I'll give some strategies to try in these situations.

CHANGING THE QUESTIONS

Many facilitators resort to memorizing the three questions of the daily meeting, losing sight of their purpose. Instead, remember the spirit behind each question. This will allow you to try other questions that promote the same focus and that do not deviate from the objective of the meeting. Such as:

1. What commitments have I fulfilled?
2. What am I committing to?
3. What obstacles do I have?

Another alternative:

1. What have I learned with what I did since the last meeting?
2. What motivates me to do what I will do before the next meeting?
3. What obstacles do I have?

Or, also:

1. What satisfactions and dissatisfactions did I have since the last daily meeting?
2. What will I do before the next meeting?
3. From 1 to 10, what probability do I think we have of achieving the objective of the sprint?

Change the Order

A factor that can contribute to the feeling of monotony in the daily meeting is to keep the same speaking order of the participants, for example, clockwise. If you add this to a certain tendency people have to sit day after day in the same place, a predictable and repetitive context is generated.

To change this behavior, I recommend to modify that order, although it may seem something too obvious or subtle. You can also try the use of a token that enables the participants to speak. When the participant that has the token finishes his/her intervention, instead of passing it to the next person, they choose who continues, gives them the element and immediately takes a step back without breaking the circle. And so it goes with each member of the team.

A different alternative that adds some fun to the meeting is to put pieces of paper with the names of the participants in a container (a pencil box, a bag, etc.) and take one name at a time to speak.

Look for Precision

Another factor that contributes to boredom during the meeting is the lack of precision from the participants. For those of us who are anxious, it is terribly frustrating to listen to people who have trouble expressing in a concrete way. Most of the examples I remember were preceded by the person thinking about what they were going to say during their turn.

To minimize this behavior, we promote the habit of preparing information before the meeting. To think "What am I going to say" only takes 5 minutes.

An alternative that I have seen in some teams is a token of around 7lb, such as a dumbbell or a rehabilitation ball. The person who receives the token holds it with arms outstretched and the time they have to speak is the time they can resist in that position (Cohn, 2012). Although it is a strategy that can be fun, I don't agree with the use of practices which can be a punishment for the members of the team. Therefore, I recommend its use only with the consent and agreement of all the participants.

Foster Collaboration

— *Since the last daily meeting, I have been sanding the legs of the chair. Before the next meeting, I'm going to glue the legs to the seat. I don't have any obstacle — said the carpenter.*

— *I have seen some colors for the fabrics of the armchairs. Before the next meeting, I'm going to choose the color. The obstacle I have is that there is no availability of the necessary color pallet until the next month. — said the upholsterer.*

— *I have measured the main hall. Before the next meeting, I'm going to calculate the amount of paint I need. The obstacle I have is that we don't know if the finish is matt or gloss — said the painter.*

— *I have been sanding the window frames. Before the next meeting, I'm going to weld the arches of the main doors. There are no obstacles — said the blacksmith.*

Are the members of this team collaborating with each other?

The lack of collaboration is evidenced in a daily meeting when each participant speaks about their work and is independent of what the other people are doing. This is the case of the people from the example: each person works on an item of the sprint backlog, the chairs, the upholstery, the painting or the enclosures.

This behavior dilutes the interest for the job that others are doing and turns the daily meeting into a sterile conversation.

This kind of situation is a symptom of a deeper cause. The recommendation, in this case, is to work with the concept of collaboration inside the team[16] and promote the work in pairs or more members of the team in each item of the sprint backlog. In this way, the tasks to be done will have more interdependence and will generate more space for collaboration.

DELEGATE TO OTHER FACILITATORS

An entertaining and challenging way, which also keeps the members of the team interested, is to offer them the possibility that each of them facilitates a daily meeting. If they want to do it, you can do a raffle, so different participants facilitate for a week and propose improvements in the meeting dynamics.

This can repeat every other week or one week per month. You can also implement it with a gradual rhythm increase so that, after a few months, they are the ones who facilitate the daily meetings without the need for a facilitator.

The only recommendation regarding this proposal is to try it after the team has been working for a reasonable amount of time to make sure they have incorporated the rhythm and habit of daily meetings.

---

[16] The topic of the collaboration in contexts of work team is posed and developed in more detail in the second book of this series, dedicated to the agile coach.

SPRINT REVIEW

The objective of the sprint review meeting is to analyze the product or service increment and, if necessary, to adapt the product backlog (Schwaber & Sutherland, 2013).

For the team and stakeholders to achieve this objective, the facilitator is responsible for promoting the following actions:

- To review the work done during the sprint.
- To obtain feedback on the work reviewed.
- To modify, if necessary, the product backlog to face future sprints.

In this way, at the end of the meeting the team will have:

- The acceptance or rejection of each of the items in the sprint backlog.
- The verification of whether they have achieved the sprint goal.
- A reviewed product backlog with new or modified items in terms of the feedback received.

ANTICIPATION

Much like the rest of agile team meetings, the work of the facilitator starts ahead of schedule. In the case of the sprint review meeting, ahead of schedule refers to the items of the sprint backlog and let the participants know that it is important that they come to the meeting.

Finished Items

Part of the work done during a sprint is to make visible if the items of the sprint backlog are finished. The agreement between the team and the stakeholders regarding what "finished" means is known as Definition of Done (*DoD*). This definition is agreed beforehand, as we have previously discussed, at the project kick-off, and it is refined in the retrospectives. This agreement is reinforced in the sprint planning meetings, and it is an essential component when it comes to deconstructing each item of the sprint backlog into tasks.

A typical definition of done expresses:

1. That the feature complies with acceptance criteria expressed and validated in the sprint planning meeting with the stakeholders.

2. That the feature has been verified and tested.

3. That the feature has not interfered negatively with other features of the product or service.

4. Ideally, that the feature can be delivered to the client and to be used (Sutherland, 2014).

To make sure that the features of the product increment are aligned with the definition of done in the sprint review meeting is also a way to make visible if the product increment is aligned with the quality agreement established with the clients.

Items Reviewed by the Product Owner

Another aspect that helps facilitate the sprint review smoothly is that the product owner reviews the product increment features in advance. Such revision could be part of the definition of done.

The fact that the product owner verifies the features built and offers feedback before the sprint review meeting fosters the collaboration with the members of the team and avoids surprises related to mistakes, misunderstandings, and adjustments which could have been mitigated with, maybe, a little effort before the sprint review, during the sprint.

PARTICIPANTS

To attend to the tasks that are typical of a review meeting (validate the achievement of the sprint goal, obtain feedback on the increment delivered and eventually, modify the product backlog), it is important that the entire team participates, that is: the product owner, the development team, the facilitator and the stakeholders (Schwaber & Sutherland, 2013).

STAKEHOLDERS

The definition presented in the Scrum Guide (Schwaber & Sutherland, 2013) does not make a distinction between the stakeholders who participate in the sprint review meeting.

In my experience, something I have seen several times and that I consider a problem is the presence of stakeholders who did not participate in the sprint planning meeting. This creates several counterproductive situations, for example, the need to allocate time to:

- Explain what the features delivered are about.
- Inform, and sometimes justify, the sprint goal.
- Explain the reasons behind the acceptance criteria of the features.
- Justify the reason why a certain feature is not part of the sprint commitment.

All these issues could have been avoided if those stakeholders had participated during the sprint planning.

In case of observing that there are people interested in attending the sprint review meeting who were not present at the sprint planning meeting, it is important that they see the records of the first meeting in advance (videos, graphics, photographs, etc.). It could also be necessary to have a previous meeting with them to clear doubts and minimize the lack of information during the sprint review meeting.

PART-TIMERS

Besides being an opportunity to validate the increment of the product or service and determine the strategy to follow based on the feedback obtained, the sprint review meeting has a second goal, which is a little bit more subtle: to foster the responsibility of the team to deliver an increment in which they had all participated.

To be present in that delivery act gives a different meaning to the work done by each member of the team. This is why, I think it is important for the members of the team who work part-time to also be present in the review meeting. This aspect is something important to protect for as long as it takes the organization to transform and promote the creation of fully dedicated teams, instead of part-time profiles.

STORYTELLING

There is nothing more boring than a sprint review meeting in which they mechanically go through each of the features built and each of the criterion of acceptance is verified. A little after the first hour, the participants start to fall asleep.

To avoid this from happening, you can make a sprint review meeting fun and attractive, involving the participants in a sort of story. For example, if you had to review the new features added to a participant enrollment process in a medicine congress, a story can be created which involves a character with a name, life history, profession and concerns. Let's read a possible story for this example:

James Summers is a surgeon from one of the provinces in the country, who wants to attend a cardiovascular surgery congress since he is there, visit the capital city with his wife and two kids.

To this effect, James completes the traditional registration fields in the form and specifies, in the companion section that he is going with an adult person called Anna Summers, and two minors called Nicholas and Florence Summers. He also indicates that he wants to extend his stay for four additional nights.

After completing these fields, the event's organization team has a consolidated report with the information of the people who will come with him. In the registration of Dr. James Summers it says that there are four people, two adults and two minors: James, Ann, Nicholas y Florence who will be staying for four nights after the congress.

When the list of attendees is handed in to the hotel administration, they will reserve a room for four people with the names of the occupants. So, when Dr. Summers does the check-in at the hotel reception desk, he will receive two electronic keys, one of them per adult.

It is ideal to arrive to the sprint review meeting with the story fully created and if possible, rehearsed. In this case, the facilitator can help the members of the team and the product owner create an engaging story beforehand.

Structure and Dynamics

Much like in the planning meeting, once the sprint review meeting started the focus of the facilitation is on the process. In order for this to be possible, it is important to make visible the aspects detailed below.

Agenda

An agenda that guides the participants in time and that is visible to everyone is useful for the review meeting to go as smoothly as possible. It is very helpful to start by checking the different items of the sprint backlog, that is, the features of the product or service increment.

Towards the end of the meeting, it is important to validate if all the participants agree with the achievement or not, of the sprint goal.

You have to be alert to prevent the review meeting from becoming –in seconds and as if by magic– a future planning meeting. If this happens, you can remind the participants of the primary objective of the meeting: review the product increment of the sprint that has just finished.

Parking Lot

As the features of the product or service increment are reviewed, the feedback will start to emerge. A good practice for it to always be visible to everyone is to record it in the parking lot. Towards the end of the review meeting, there could be a timeframe dedicated to reviewing all the feedback registered and to decide in what way it modifies the product backlog in the future.

Review of the Features

Many people know the review meeting as "demo meeting". I never liked that name because I think that it gives a feeling of formal meeting, where the team shows the increment of product to a quiet group of stakeholders who later give their opinions.

There can be different levels of feedback in a meeting. To analyze them, I will base on an example. Let's imagine that our product is a wedding party. In this sprint, we have built a product increment that entails 1) the chairs, 2) the tablecloths and 3) the entrée of the party. Now, let's analyze the possible levels of feedback:

Feedback Level 0: the team presents the features of the new increment of the product. They use a projector to show the blueprints of the design, the photos of the chairs, the technical descriptions of the tablecloth's fabric composition, a close up photo of the tablecloth that is going to be used, the recipe and the preparation procedure of the entrée. At the end, the stakeholders **give their opinion on what they imagined based on what they saw**.

Feedback Level 1: The team gives a presentation as they use the features of the new increment of the product. This means that, as they tell the stakeholders about the new features of the increment –a very comfortable chair and with proper height, the texture of the tablecloth which is quite soft, an excellent meat dish, etc.-, the members of the team sit on the chairs, use the tablecloth and try the entrée. At the end, the stakeholders give their **opinion on what they saw and heard**.

Feedback Level 2: The team involves the interested parties in a story in which they are the protagonists and where they use the features of the new increment of the product. The interested parties perform different roles in the story: one is the groom, the other is the bride, and the rest can be the family and the guests. The meeting room is decorated with chairs and the tablecloths that are going to be evaluated. The stakeholders sit on the chairs and touch the tablecloths. As they see them, they give their opinion on the adjustments they would do and what they are discovering at that moment. Try the food (this time the meeting was organized at lunchtime). By the end, the stakeholders, give their **opinion on what they lived and experienced**.

The goal is that the sprint review meeting generates and facilitates a feedback level 2. Here, storytelling plays a vital role as well as the involvement of the stakeholders in the use of the increment of the product.

The Sprint Goal

After reviewing all the features committed for the product or service increment, and before closing the review, it is important to verify if the goal proposed for this sprint has been achieved.

Redesigning the Product Backlog and the Delivery Plan

The result of the review of the product or service increment can redefine the future product backlog.

Towards the end of the review meeting, it is advised to review all the feedback recorded in the parking lot, together with the adjustments that need to be done on the future features, product of the learning process and the discovery of the result and user experience.

Any change that comes up could be measured at a high level by the members of the team to review and reconsider possible adjustments to the future delivery plan. It is important to explicit that, at his instance, the modifications in the delivery dates are tentative and are subject to a detailed review to be done by the entire team.

ASKING FOR HELP

An aspect that I would add after reading the book *Coaching Agile Teams* by *Lyssa Adkins* and that I encourage in spring review meetings is the possibility to ask the stakeholders for help.

Lyssa proposes this as the objective of every review meeting. When the team poses the obstacles they need help with, barriers that no member of the team -including the product owner and the facilitator- can solve, you can take advantage of the review meeting to ask the interested parties to help them solve such obstacles.

PLANNING RETROSPECTIVE

As it happens in all sessions, especially those with stakeholders, at the end I recommend doing a quick retrospective that allows the detection of improvements to be done at the next meeting. To do that, you can apply any of the dynamics mentioned for the retrospective of the project kick-off meeting.

Sprint Retrospective

At the end of each sprint, the team meets in a retrospective. This meeting is an opportunity for the team to review their actions and create an improvement plan that will be carried out in the next sprint. (Schwaber & Sutherland, 2013).

For the team to achieve its goal during the retrospective, the facilitator is responsible for promoting and facilitating the following actions:

- Review the way in which the work was carried out during the sprint.
- Identify and prioritize the strengths and opportunities for improvement.
- Plan the addition of improvements in the way the team performs their job.

At the end of this meeting, the team should have an improvement plan for the next sprint.

Anticipation

At this point in the book, one can say that we agree on how important it is to anticipate in the facilitation of all the meetings.

The work of the facilitator of a retrospective also starts beforehand. In this case, the focus will be on the analysis of how the team itself performs their work.

Improvement Opportunities

Wherever one or more people are working together, there will also be improvement opportunities. Either the place where the meeting was held could be improved, or the chairs the team uses, the temperature of the work space, the way a particular activity is being performed, the format in which the people receive information or the relationship that exists between certain people. There is always room for growth.

The work of the facilitator of a team consists of not losing sight of those opportunities for improvement.

To foster this visibility and consideration, I have seen something that works very well is to have a permanent space near the team where to propose and record visible problems and possible improvements. It would be a kind of suggestion box, with the difference that here the ideas are visible to everyone and that, besides suggestions, you can record problems without any suggested solution, which allows for the proposal to emerge from the team during the retrospective.

This gathering can be done with a board and some sticky notes.

Participants

As the retrospective meeting goal is to look for better ways to do the job in the future, it is important that the product owner participates as well as the construction team and the facilitator.

Part-timers

As I have mentioned in previous pages, in an agile organization the tendency is not to have part-time profiles in the projects. That means we avoid the people who work on multiple projects at the same time. We are interested in having teams of people who are very focused on a particular product.

The road to this scenario is usually very long and, as long as the objective is not achieved, it is important to learn to live with those part-time team members. The people who work part-time in the project tend to be taken into account much the same as the other members of the team. They participate in all the meetings, including the retrospective.

Product Owner

The participation of the product owner in the retrospective is one of the most discussed controversies in the Scrum community worldwide.

In the first years of Scrum, the product owner did not participate in this meeting. The final meeting of each sprint is reserved just for the work team and the Scrum Master or facilitator. The reason behind this decision was the need for a safe and secure space where the team can express freely, without censorship or fears.

As time passed, a new school of thought appeared that sees the product owner part of the team and considers that the lack of a safe space in presence of the product owner is due to a lack of trust in the relationships between the parts, which makes it an obstacle to be solved.

I agree with this last approach, which considers the product owner a member of the team, and, therefore, I foster his/her participation in the retrospective meetings. I think future improvements are a concern of the members of the team, the facilitator, and the product owner, as long as they entail a review and adaptation process at the level of the entire team.

Themes

Lyssa Adkins[17] suggests the use of themes in retrospectives.

To this end, the facilitator observes, during the sprint, which could be the biggest problems the team is going through and, as the retrospective draws near, analyze his/her list of observations. Maybe a theme or two come to light. In this case, the facilitator can choose one of them as the main theme of the meeting. In turn, I recommend you verify that choice with a couple of members of the team and the product owner to know your perspectives. What have they seen in this sprint? What are they curious about? What is bothering them?

Structure and Dynamics

Once the retrospective has started, the focus of the facilitation is on the conversation. For this to be possible, it is necessary to make the aspects I present below visible.

Agenda

If we had to choose a single reference when we talk about retrospectives, to me it would be the book *Agile Retrospectives, Making Good Teams Great* by Diana Larsen and Esther Derby[18].

The authors propose an agenda, which consists of five stages:

1) Prepare the scenario.

---

[17] Adkins, 2010. Ob Cit.

[18] LARSEN, D., DERBY, E., Agile Retrospectives: Making Good Teams Great, PragPub, 2006

2) Gather data.

3) Generate a deeper understanding.

4) Decide what to do.

5) Closure.

This structure proposal is developed in the book mentioned above. For this reason, we will not expand on these topics.

Whatever agenda structure is chosen, it is important that it is visible to everyone. I recommend the use of some element, such as, a sticky note, to mark the moment of the agenda that they are currently going through.

As we have already mentioned, the agenda is not written in stone and therefore, it is not necessary to follow it to a T. It only represents a safe place where to go back to if the conversations divert. Once the agenda is visible, it lets the conversation do its job.

Independently of the agenda created, the things that people worry about tend to emerge. So, it is not necessary to worry too much about the agenda preventing it. If the members of the team are worried, they will find the way to make these worries visible, regardless of what has been planned. (Adkins, 2010)

I have used the structure proposed by Larsen and Derby over the years, and recently I have been adding and testing something I thought was missing for the retrospective to be a moment of more awareness for the team: the review of improvement commitments assumed in previous retrospectives.

The addition I keep doing modifies the agenda in the following way:

1) Prepare the scenario.
2) **Review of committed improvements (new).**
3) Gather information.
4) Generate a deeper understanding.

5) Decide what to do.
6) Closure.

Soon, I will tell you about how important is to me the review of committed improvements. Before that, I think it is necessary to emphasize two vital aspects that usually take place when preparing the scenario: reconfirm the objective of the retrospective and highlight the prime directive.

Goal of the Retrospective

As it is explained at the beginning of this section, the goal of the retrospective is that the team reviews its actions and creates an improvement plan to be carried out during the next sprint.

Regardless of how clear the objective is, many teams do not only diverge from the agenda following its own concerns (that is quite common and it is not necessary to prevent it emphatically), but also transform the retrospective into another kind of meeting. For example, it is usual for the members of the team to end up talking about the features of the product or service, as if it were a sprint meeting.

To avoid this, the first step is to explicitly reconfirm the objective of the retrospective at the beginning. You can hang the objective on a wall, so it is visible for all the participants and point at it whenever necessary, and invite the entire team to resume it and refocus the conversation.

Prime Directive

Prime directive is an affirmation that leads the people to a collaborative frame of mind. It is a belief that the team supports during the activities that constitute the retrospective. (Kerth, 2001)

Prime directive expresses that, independently of what we discover, understand and truly believe, each person did their best, given what they knew at the moment, their abilities, available resources and the situation in particular.

You can take advantage of the beginning of the retrospective, that is, the preparation stage of the scenario, to write the prime directive in a visible way for all the participants and generate the verbal commitment of all the people involved to respect it and support it during the meeting.

The prime directive can also be recorded in a visible way and left during the whole meeting, to be pointed at whenever it is necessary.

REVIEW OF COMMITTED IMPROVEMENTS

Before beginning to analyze the sprint that has just finished, I recommend allocating a period of time to evaluate the outcomes of the committed improvements in the previous sprint retrospective. This will help all the team in two aspects:

- Corroborate the effectiveness of the decisions and actions chosen to carry out the improvements.

- Reconfirm the commitment on the improvement actions selected in the previous sprint.

Regarding the second item, when the teams don't review the outcomes of the improvements actions chosen in the previous sprint, it is common that they lose relevance. This leads the entire team not to improve significantly and that the meeting transforms into a catharsis of recurring problems.

Inspect and Adapt

Having reviewed past actions and their results, it is now time to analyze the sprint that is finishing, to explore improvement points and leverage them.

I don't need to think much to, again, strongly recommend the book *Agile Retrospectives, Making Good Teams Great* where you can find many techniques and activities for the remaining phases of the proposed structure for the retrospective meeting:

- Gather information
- Generate a deeper understanding
- Deciding what to do

New Definition of Done

A decision that is many times forgotten in retrospectives, is to review and eventually modify the definition of done that the team has.

After each sprint review, there will be a lot of valuable information regarding the quality perspective of the stakeholders and the members of the team have about the increment in the product or service. The idea is to capitalize this information and redefine the agreement on what it means when something is done, especially, in those cases where the quality increment of the product or service, is not enough to cover the expected level.

Closure

Once the structure of the retrospective has been finished, you enter the last stage, the closure: an opportunity for continuous improvement, to think about what happened during the meeting and express gratitude (Larsen & Derby, 2006).

A space to acknowledge the members of the team creates a positive ending for the retrospective. To this effect, you can invite each member of the team to thank something valuable that they consider the other one did to help him/her or the team, in the retrospective as well as during the sprint.

Towards the end, you can dedicate a few minutes to explore and improve the meeting: it would be a retrospective of the retrospective. To do that, you can use any of the dynamics mentioned in chapter 6.

After the Retrospective

The work of the facilitator does not finish when the retrospective finishes. Although that space of reflection closes temporarily, the responsibility of the person who facilitates continues in the new sprint.

It is important and motivating for the team to continually see the advance of the chosen improvement tasks in the retrospective for the next sprint. To do that, you can use a task board and allow the members of the team to be the ones that keep it up to date.

This small action contributes to the awareness of the team that, apart from the creation of the increment of the product or service, its job also involves continuous improvement.

MEETING THE EXPERTS
HIROSHI HIROMOTO

Hiroshi Hiromoto is an Agile Coach & Trainer at Kleer, facilitator and Kata Geek. As well as passionate about the continuous improvement.

🐦 *@hhiroshi*

In my experience as an agile coach, the activity I have done the most is the facilitation of retrospectives. I have facilitated retrospectives in different contexts such as banking, sales, marketing, finance, software development, and business ventures; and with various amounts of participants, from 3 people up to 48 people. In this work experience, I have had multiple learnings, but if I had to share only one of them, I would undoubtedly choose *hansei's* application.

Hansei is a Japanese word whose closest translation is introspection or reflection. The first time that I heard the word *hansei* was when I was approximately 5 or 6 years old. At that time I used to spend a lot of time at my grandparent's house (who are Japanese) and every time I behaved badly my grandfather would say *hansei-shinasai* (do *hansei*), expecting me to think about what I had just done. Later on, in my school and university life, I stopped going to their house as often, but that word remained stuck in my memories, and it wasn't until many years later while I was reading about Toyota, that I came across it again, explained as a vital step for improvement.

To understand the benefit of doing *hansei* in a retrospective, it is necessary to understand that in the Japanese culture *hansei* is not just an individual action (as I did as a child) but also collective, in particular, many organizations in Japan usually have something called *hansei-kai*, which could be translated as meetings to do *hansei*. In these meetings, the problematics that emerged are analyzed (sometimes they are also called for a particular problem) where each participant reflects collectively on how he/she could have done things to avoid the problem regardless of their responsibility. And it is precisely at this point where *hansei-kai* differs from the usual post-mortem meetings we usually have.

To explain it more clearly I am going to tell you an anecdote of a friend of mine who works in a software development company in Japan.

In one of the products they were developing arose a serious problem in production, which prevented a third of their users from accessing the application. After solving the incident, the team called a *hansei-kai*. Once they were all together, the meeting started with the boss summarizing the incident and later asked what each of them thought they had failed at and how they could avoid it in the future. Based on the question, each member of the team started to answer from their own perspective (without blaming anyone, without giving excuses). At the end of the meeting, the boss wrote down the lessons learned and sent them via e-mail closing the session.

How does this apply to retrospectives? Well if we remember that the purpose of a retrospective is for the team to reflect on how to be more effective to later adjust and perfect its behavior in consequence (agile principle), *hansei* is a very effective way to generate that reflection without falling into common anti-patterns such as the tendency to victimize yourself or the blame game, and on the other hand to reinforce the thought that "in this team, no problem is somebody else's problem".

So, I recommend you, in your next retrospective, that at the moment of analyzing a problem, you invite the participants to think about What could I have done differently to avoid this issue?

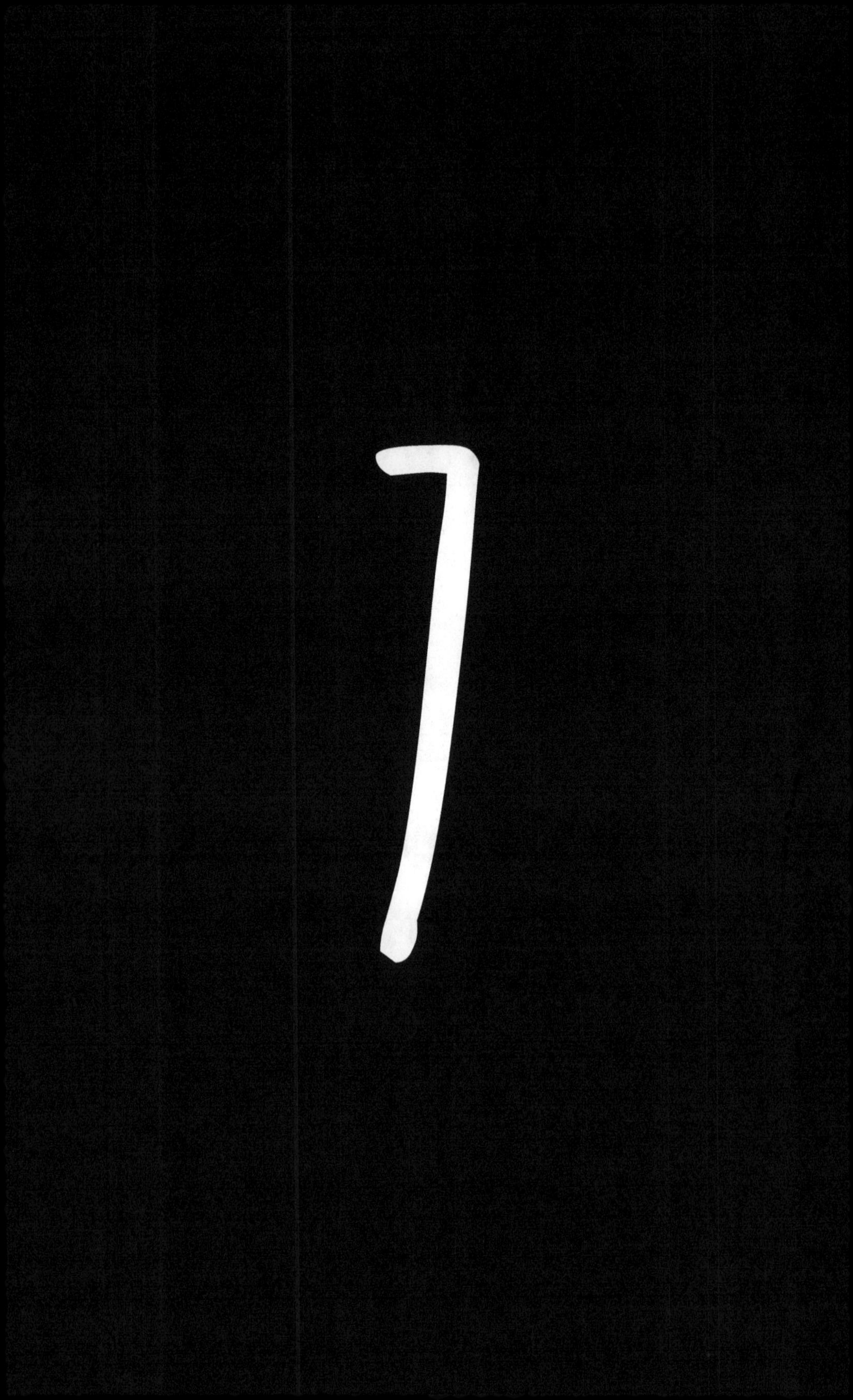

Agile Team Facilitator Development

One of my most cherished childhood memories is the first time I traveled by plane. I was seven years old, and I was with my father watching the planes take off and land at the local city airport. The next thing I remember is my dad buying a round ticket to a nearby city for the day. He had decided to give me that experience just for the experience itself.

We went on that flight. The whole round trip must have taken around four hours. I got off that plane determined to become a pilot.

The time passed and during the last year of high school I made some inquiries to start studying to become and Aeronautical Engineer. The program included subjects such as Aerodynamics, Propulsion, Flight Mechanics and Flight Regulations, etc. It was love at first sight.

I found out there was a career guidance talk in one of the universities that provided that major and I decided to attend. The conference included many interesting topics and towards the end, I interviewed one of the Aeronautical Engineers who had graduated two years before.

It was such a huge surprise when I discovered that that an Aeronautical Engineer did not know how to fly a plane. But how Aeronautical Engineers don't know how to fly? The answer to this question was "not necessarily". Some, on their own, train to become Plane Pilots, which is completely independent from their Aeronautical Engineering training.

When I discovered this, I decided not to become an Aeronautical Engineer: I wanted to be a Plane Pilot. However, there was one question I couldn't get out of my head: How is it possible that an Aeronautical Engineer does not know how to fly a plane since they know so much about the matter?

Years later, when I was actually training to become a pilot, I discovered the answer to that question: to know about something doesn't mean you know how to do it.

I learned that during my second flying session. During the first session, the instructor had landed the plane, and on that occasion, he told me that the next time it would be me the one to do it.

I had very few days, and I researched about how the landing happened on a plane. At the end of the day, it was a matter of aerodynamics, a process where the pilot modifies the attitude of the plane (the wing's angle of attack), going from a *nose down* attitude to a *nose up* which will happen at the moment the wheels touch the runway. During that process, the aircraft loses speed and therefore sustenance, until it is only affirmed by its wheels. With more detail than what I include here, I arrived to my second flying lesson, having thoroughly studied the process of landing.

We went up to a thousand feet of altitude (approximately 300 meters), and we started to do some flight maneuvers. After an hour of work, the instructor told me to head for the airport we had departed from: I was going to do my first landing. It was about a 10-minute flight until we got to the airport. During that time, I mentally reviewed all the steps I had studied in detail about the landing process. I felt confident; I remembered each and every one of them. I was ready...or so I thought.

I aligned the plane with the runway and started the descent. The speed was within the expected parameters. I was very close to achieving it, I passed the runway threshold, and the wheels were already less than ten feet above the ground. It was time to change progressively the plane attitude to start losing speed and sustenance.

So I did: I raised the nose of the plane, and the plane went up, how did it go up!!?? Then I lowered the nose, gained speed, no! I raised the nose. The plane went up again. No! Lower and more speed. This time, I hit the wheels with the runway and bounced like a basketball. It went up again, down again, and bounced again. Meanwhile, the plane started to tilt towards the left. And for this reason, when I bounced a third time, the left wheel hit the ground first and then the right wheel. At this point, I think I had completely lost control. The instructor sitting next to me took the controls of the aircraft and in five seconds leveled it and landed the plane caressing the runway.

But... what had happened to me!? I had a first-hand experience with the learning process: to know about something, in my case, the landing of a plane, does not guarantee that you know how to do that, in my case, landing the plane correctly.

TO KNOW ABOUT SOMETHING DOES NOT IMPLY KNOWING HOW TO DO THAT.

To know how to do something you need to go through a learning process that goes beyond the simple knowledge of the subject and which involves the continuous practice and the development of your own abilities.

This process is necessary for all disciplines, including facilitation.

The proposal of this chapter is to explore a possible learning process that we will later apply to the discipline of facilitating an agile team.

FROM NOVICE TO EXPERT

In the same way, the pilot of a plane becomes an expert through practice, a facilitator of agile teams also goes on that road. Let's take a look at the model to develop abilities that Dreyfus presents (Dreyfus & Dreyfus, 1986). This model discusses the different stages of a learning process.

Stage 1: Novice

The learning process starts with the apprentice following to a T the rules that the instructor has systematized and transmitted. He will interact with the different elements that are useful for his task, but which have been presented isolated from the context, and as a pre-established set of rules and regulations to perform an action that does not depend on external variables. In this way, the novice conceptualizes and begins to operate in a simple and direct manner, without too many complications.

The novice plane pilot comes close to the ground during the landing and pulls the command to raise the nose. Something that according to his instinct could manifest itself as a contradiction (I want to go down but instead I am raising the nose of the plane). He will pay attention to the speed, to the control of the plane, to the indicator of the flaps position. He will not know how high to raise the nose, at what precise moment or how fast he should do it. He is only doing it because there is an instructor beside him who gives him instructions. Some novice pilots even push the plane command to lower the nose, which seems instinctive to them but many times can cause an accident if the instructor is distracted.

The novice facilitator of agile teams will use the techniques and tools exactly as they have been presented; he will follow the meeting agenda to a T, without diverting not even an ounce from what was pre-established. In many cases, he will follow his instinct and without noticing, he will intervene in the content of the conversations and decisions of the teams. At this stage of his learning process, he will not necessarily take into consideration the context to modify the practice.

Stage 2: Advanced Beginner

As the advanced beginner goes through real experiences, he starts to identify additional significant aspects of each situation. After a few similar consecutive experiences, the novice incorporates those situational aspects as parameters which can be taken into account to alter the practice.

The advanced beginner plane pilot incorporates the attitude of the plane at a particular regime of propeller rotation as an indication of the acceleration or deceleration of the airplane.

The agile team facilitator in his advanced beginner stage starts to identify the situational aspects such as the people's mood, emotions, gestures and the different types of conversations as indicators of the need to change the direction of the agenda or the activities and acts accordingly.

The advanced beginner admits that he needs the support of a mentor and that, in case he is left alone, can see himself involved in situations he does not yet know how to solve.

Stage 3: Competent

When his experience increases so does the number of variable situations that the advanced beginner can identify. Sooner or later, the number of situational aspects at stake become overwhelming for the person who is going through the learning process. At that moment, he can question his ability to dominate them all.

By accepting his limitation, the advanced beginner develops an ability for situational prioritization: in a specific situation, he identifies which are the important factors and which are those that can be ignored. By restricting the amount of variables, he accelerates the decision-making process to create an action plan and goes ahead with it.

When a competent plane pilot is landing, he can identify the direction of the wind, the horizontal and vertical position of his plane in relation to the glide slope to the runway, its speed, etc. Based on those parameters he will decide whether he decreases the power or not, raises or lowers the nose of the plane, increases or reduces the degrees of the flaps. He will feel relieved if the plane corrects its angle and approximation speed and upset if it doesn´t.

The competent agile team facilitator in a sprint planning meeting can identify the mood of the stakeholders and the members of the team, the confidence that the team feels for achieving its commitments, the pressure level that the stakeholders can be imprinting on the situation, the time the conversations take, the participant's level of general involvement, etc. In this way, he decides if he increases or reduces the rhythm, invites a pause or not, facilitates an in-depth analysis of the subjects or not, generates a sharing session or new divergence instance, etc. He will feel relieved if his actions produce the expected outcomes and will be upset if they don't.

At this stage, the apprentice manages to perform in normal or expected situations. He is not yet able to face unexpected or emergency situations. An example of this is when the flying instructor tells his student: "in case of a real emergency, the plane is mine". This happens until the flight student reaches a significant level of dexterity.

At this point of the learning process, the Dreyfuses make a key distinction that will determine the future of the apprentice regarding the process he is going through:

1. If the apprentice commits emotionally more and more with the task, he will move away from that disregarded attitude of the context, where the focus was on following the rules. This implies that the person will be in a better position to achieve a higher development of their abilities.
2. If the apprentice feels inhibited due to the responsibility that taking risks involves, he can get stuck in his learning process.

Stage 4: Proficient

The competent beginner has committed emotionally with the activity. At this point of the learning process, intuition starts to replace theory. The Dreyfuses are radical at this point: the skill seems to develop only if the experience is assimilated in a practical way and the intuition replaces the reasoned answers.

The action becomes easier and less worrying. The person who is learning starts to identify what he needs to achieve instead of what needs to be done. He no longer drowns in a logical process of variable evaluation and reasoned decision-making. At this stage of the learning process, doubts begin to dissipate about how correct it is to do what needs to be.

Here the apprentice senses what he needs to achieve and then resorts to the different courses of action to choose whichever he considers more appropriate.

The proficient plane pilot senses that his approximation speed is too low, so he conscientiously chooses whether to lower the nose of the plane or increase the power.

The proficient facilitator detects the missing conversations or the underlying conflicts in the interactions among members of the team, and between them and the stakeholders. In this way, he decides the rhythm, the way, and the activities he will include during the facilitation.

STAGE 5: EXPERT

The expert just knows what to do. Besides intuitively detecting a situation, he also senses the necessary actions.

The Dreyfuses say that, to the expert, what needs to be done simply gets done.

The expert plane pilot responds intuitively to a gust of wind that takes him by surprise during the landing. The aircraft moves from side to side while the expert pilot executes the commands with a frenzy, but his face and body look calm and collected. To the expert pilot, that situation simply gets solved. Many times he's unable to explain how he did it.

The expert facilitator has incorporated this discipline as part of his action, and having expanded his abilities, he facilitates the meetings, conversations and the decision-making processes while detecting, at the same time, where and how he should intervene following his intuition.

SELF-ASSESSMENT

Based on the different levels of the learning process proposed by the Dreyfuses, I propose a self-assessment model. The idea is that you use it along your career as an agile team facilitator.

The self-assessment is divided into different areas that you need to consider and explore:

- Responsibilities of the agile team facilitator
- Design and structure of the meetings.
- Graphic recording and facilitation.
- Facilitation of collaborative processes.
- Facilitation of the agile project kick-off.
- Facilitation of the sprint planning.
- Facilitation of the daily meeting.
- Facilitation of the sprint review
- Facilitación de la retrospectiva.

Each one of these areas is divided into different aspects.

I propose that you to assign a number from 0 to 5, with each number representing the level of learning process where you think you are regarding that aspect.

After assigning the values, it will be necessary for you to calculate the corresponding average for each area.

That average will indicate the stage of the learning process where you are regarding that specific area of the facilitation.

I recommend you to have this reference at hand while you answer the self-evaluation:

0: Ignorant

I have no knowledge about this aspect or what it refers to.

1: Novice

I only consider myself capable of executing this aspect if I follow the instructions. The degree of autonomy I have in this domain is null. I depend on the guidelines which include the steps that indicate how to proceed.

2: Advanced Beginner

I'm acquiring the necessary competences in this domain. I'm aware that I still can't execute effectively. The degree of autonomy I have is limited.

3: Competent

I feel comfortable but look for supervision when facing unexpected or emergency situations. Except these especial cases, I can take responsibility for the situations in an autonomous way.

4: Proficient

I'm autonomous; I don't need direct guidance or supervision. I'm familiar with the challenges than can arise. I know how to anticipate and how to deal with them when they appear. I'm considered as a referent by those who do not perform in this domain. I produce results. I act with a small degree of deliverance; I could say I get into a flow state. Only the unexpected situations interrupt that flow. I have developed a sense of responsibility for my actions and for the product of such actions.

5: Expert

I execute with little or no deliverance. My actions seem like a dance. There is little interruption, and when unexpected challenges arise, I have resources at hand. I establish execution standards in the domain and my actions are imitated by others. Besides doing what needs to be done, I add my own personal style to my work.

How do I look?

Responsibilities of the agile team facilitator

Aspect	Score
I honor the dialogue over the monologue, the exchange of ideas and that group conversations maintain their sense.	
I help the participants establish and respect their work agreements.	
I deconstruct large or complex topics into smaller and more manageable ones.	
I accompany the participants to navigate through the conflicts that arise in the team.	
I coordinate conversations; especially those with many participants so that the fluency is not lost, maintain the sense and achieve the results proposed.	
Every time the input of a participant is not clear for the rest of the team, I paraphrase it and help clarify the message.	
I use flipcharts, posters, drawings and other resources to make information as well as the decision making process visible.	
I offer an adequate space, of trust and with the characteristics required to carry out the work dynamics chosen for each situation.	

I am aware of the participant's emotions and the changes in the team's mood.	
I anticipate to the team meetings, generating connection activities, identifying possible work dynamics and establishing the corresponding agenda to the type of meeting and the subjects to discuss.	
I procure the optimal spatial conditions and the resources necessary for the team meetings.	
I communicate my change of role explicitly if at any moment I think it is necessary to intervene in the content or the result of the team conversations.	
I delegate the facilitation to somebody else if I see myself intervening too often in the content or the result of team conversations.	
I create a space where all the participants have the chance to express themselves and I check that the other members have heard and understood.	
I foster the use of all the available resources by all participants when it comes to facilitating a group conversation: flipcharts, sticky notes, sheets of paper, tape, etc.	

I use all the space available when facilitating a group conversation: the participants stand up, draw, form groups, share conclusions, use posters, etc.	
I leave attractive evidence of the meetings and conversations I facilitate.	
Promedio:	

MEETING DESIGN AND STRUCTURE

Aspect	Score
I do research in advance to identify the real needs of the team.	
I present an agenda and a series of dynamics that all the members of the team know and understand.	
I make sure the meetings and conversations I facilitate have a clear objective, and it is known to everyone.	
I make the agenda visible so that the participants always know where they are standing, the topics we have discussed and what still needs to be done.	
I divert from the meeting agenda if I consider it necessary. I know when to leave it and when to come back.	

I maintain the focus of the conversations and separate the emergent topics to deal with them at the end of the meeting or later on.	
I give enough entity to closing the meeting so that the participants feel empowered and motivated for action when they leave.	
Average:	

GRAPHIC RECORDING AND FACILITATION

Aspect	Score
I differentiate graphic documentation from graphic facilitation and use each of them when they are pertinent and necessary.	
I use different graphic elements to maximize understanding of the conversation and the possibilities to obtain shared interpretations.	
I use simple, quick, graphic representations to facilitate the reading and understanding of the topics discussed in the meeting.	
After finishing, I send them the graphic evidence (visual minutes) as a differentiating element of the meetings I facilitate.	
Average:	

FACILITATION OF COLLABORATIVE PROCESSES

Aspect	Score
I facilitate complex participative decision-making processes.	
I differentiate the stages of divergence, groan and convergence of a participative decision-making process.	
I use different tools that foster the participation during the divergence stage.	
I use tools and techniques which facilitate the conversation during the groan stage.	
I use decision-making tools and techniques that facilitate the convergence stage of the teams.	
I facilitate the creation of shared agreements after a participative decision-making process.	
Average:	

KICK-OFF FACILITATION OF AN AGILE PROJECT

Aspect	Score
I design attractive and powerful invitations for agile project kick-off meetings.	
I make sure all the key participants are present in the project kick-off meeting and help them, if necessary, for this to happen.	

I ensure and transmit the importance of being punctual in agile project kick-off meetings.	
I make tools and techniques available to the team that help them establish clear objectives and a shared vision about what needs to be achieved.	
I use dynamics that help the participants identify the community of stakeholders of the project that is starting.	
I provide tools for the participants to establish clarity about the product or service that they are attempting to create.	
I facilitate the identification of the high-level scope (what they should and shouldn't do).	
I transmit techniques and tools that allow them to associate the features of the new product or service with the business objectives.	
I help all the participants to leave this project kick-off meeting with a clear and shared understanding of the scope priorities.	
I promote conversations among the participants to identify risks, dimensioning the work and creating agreements about the quality expectations of the deliverables.	
I create spaces for reflection to improve daily in case the workshops take several days.	
Average:	

FACILITATION OF THE SPRINT PLANNING

Aspect	Score
I work closely with the product owner to guarantee a constantly detailed, estimated, emergent and prioritized backlog (DEEP).	
I make sure I increase the awareness of the PO so that the higher priority items of the product backlog comply with the INVEST features: independent, negotiable, valuable for the business, estimatable, small and testable.	
I help the PO so that the items of the product backlog presented in the sprint planning meeting comply with the Definition of Ready (DoR).	
I allocate time for all the people necessary to plan a sprint participate in the planning meeting.	
I ensure that the product backlog is available for the stakeholders so all the team can check it at any moment.	
I guarantee that each sprint has a clear objective which is known to everyone.	
I promote the dialogue between the stakeholders and the team until they reach a shared understanding about the commitments of the sprint.	
I help the team deconstruct each item of the product backlog in tasks and create a high-level plan for the sprint.	

I raise awareness in the team about how important it is to start each sprint with a high-level design/agreement.	
Average:	

FACILITATION OF A DAILY MEETING

Aspect	Score
I promote a space of mutual understanding and synchronization during the daily meetings.	
I prepare dynamics that help the members of the team maintain the focus during the meeting.	
I guarantee the compliance with the time-box of the daily meeting.	
I intervene when it is necessary to prevent the meeting from becoming a status report.	
I raise awareness in the team about the inconvenience of altering the scope of the sprint during the daily meeting.	
Me ocupo de generar reuniones diarias entretenidas, variadas y atractivas para los miembros del equipo.	
Average:	

FACILITATION OF THE SPRINT REVIEW

Aspect	Score
I help he members of the team so the items of the product backlog presented in the sprint review comply with the Definition of Done (*DoD*).	
I make sure the product owner reviews the items of the *product backlog* before the review meeting.	
I allocate time so that all the people necessary to review the sprint participate in the review meeting.	
I make sure that the review meetings of the sprint are entertaining and attractive for all the participants.	
I promote the stakeholders' involvement by letting them use the product or service during the sprint review meeting.	
I encourage help requests that the team needs to make the stakeholders during the planning meetings or the sprint review.	
I make sure that the objective of the sprint is taken into consideration when it is time to review the results of the sprint.	
Average:	

FACILITATION OF THE RETROSPECTIVE

Aspect	Score
I encourage the team to anticipate the detection of improvement opportunities before each retrospective	
I allocate time for the participation of all the necessary individuals during the retrospective meetings.	
I create an environment of trust, openness and respect during the retrospectives so that the members of the team feel safe to express themselves without feeling afraid.	
I use different techniques and tools to facilitate retrospectives and I rotate them to avoid monotony.	
I ensure the review of the committed improvements in previous retrospectives in each team retrospective	
I help the members of the team know and take into consideration the prime directive in each retrospective.	
I guarantee the review and if necessary, the redefinition of the definition of done (*DoD*) in each retrospective.	

I make the commitments assumed visible and available to everyone in each retrospective after each meeting finishes.	
Average:	

Taking into consideration the averages of each self-evaluation area, which ones do you think are those areas you consider you need to acquire a higher level of competence?

I recommend you to complete this self-evaluation at least once a month and have a record of your progress. If you decidedly pay attention to those areas you believe you need to improve, before you know it you will be performing as a facilitator of agile teams at a proficient or expert level.

Closing

The Next Step

This book is dedicated to the first step in the professional development of an agile coach in Entrepreneurial Agility, which is precisely facilitating agile teams.

As it was explained in the prologue of this book, the conception of career is inspired in the road to development[19] proposed by the International Consortium for Agility (ICAgile) according to which the facilitator of agile teams can facilitate one or two agile teams and is not qualified to pursue an initiative of Agile transformation.

As I conceive the professional road in this discipline, two roads are open for development: one is towards agile coaching and the other one towards the agile trainer.

Development towards agile coaching

The next step on the road towards agile coaching consists of the transformation of an agile team facilitator into a coach. An agile coach is a facilitator who has reached an expert level and at the same time has developed professional coaching abilities. The agile coach works with multiple teams, and starts-up new teams, offers mentoring to facilitators of agile teams and promotes a broader outlook of the organization.

---

[19]ICAgile – Agile Coaching Track

Development towards agile training and education

This road includes the evolution of the expert facilitator of agile teams who has developed abilities of adult training, participative education and management of large learning groups.

We will cover both roads with the consecutive books of this series

Coming to the end of this book, I would like to share a fragment of the book "The Teachings of Don Juan", by Carlos Castaneda, who has made an impression in my professional life after becoming acquainted with agility and coaching. This passage is known as "A path with a heart" and it goes like this:

"... Anything is one of a million paths. Therefore, you must always keep in mind that a path is only a path; if you feel you should not follow it, you must not stay with it under any conditions. To have such clarity you must lead a disciplined life. Only then will you know that any path is only a path and there is no affront, to oneself or to others, in dropping it if that is what your heart tells you to do. (...)

Look at every path closely and deliberately. Try it as many times as you think necessary. Then ask yourself, and you alone, a question:

Does this path have a heart?

If it does, the path is good; if it doesn't, it is of no use. All paths are the same: they lead nowhere. They are paths going through the bush. No path leads nowhere, but one has a heart, the other doesn't. One makes for a joyful journey; as long as you follow it, you are one with it. The other will make you curse your life. One makes you strong; the other weakens you

The trouble is nobody asks the question, and when a man finally realizes that he has taken a path without a heart, the path is ready to kill him. A path without a heart is never enjoyable. You

have to work hard even to take it. At that point, few people can stop to think and leave the road

On the other hand, a path with heart is easy: it does not make you work at liking it. For me there is only the traveling on paths that have heart, on any path that may have heart. That's how I travel, and the only challenge worthwhile is to traverse its full length-- and there I travel looking, looking breathlessly".

So, you, agile team facilitator who intend to follow the road towards Enterprise Agility Coaching, ask yourself this question whenever you can:

DOES THIS PATH HAVE A HEART?

Thanks for having got this far!

Martín.

ABOUT THE AUTHOR

My name is Martin. I feel strongly attracted to the human side of teams and organizational behaviour. I am a Certified Professional Coach, Certified Scrum Trainer (CST) and Certified Enterprise Coach (CEC). I had the chance of having worked with clients of all sizes in America and Europe. I am a frequent speaker and facilitator of sessions in various international conferences on Agile and Scrum.

I'm passionate about human relationships, participatory and transformational learning, and self-organization. My attention is currently focused on coaching, both at the executive level and at the enterprise level, and creating environments where individuals learn the most and challenge themselves.

In June 2009, I founded Kleer, a company of which I am part today. Alongside professionals who I admire, in a daily basis, we conduct our business with the aim to promote and accompany other organizations in their transformation to new and more effective ways of working, innovate and interact with customers.

In order to know more about me, I invite you to visit my blog: http://www.martinalaimo.com/en/

References

Adkins, L. (2010). *Coaching Agile Teams.* Addison-Wesley Professional.

Adzic, G. (2012). *Impact Mapping: Making a big impact with software products and projects.* Provoking Thoughts.

Alaimo, M. (2013). *Equipos Más Productivos.* Kleer.

Alaimo, M., & Salias, M. (2015). *Proyectos Ágiles con Scrum: Flexibilidad, aprendizaje, innovación y colaboración en contextos complejos* (2 ed.). Kleer.

Behrens, P. (2011). *Applying to Become a CSC.* Retrieved from Scrum Alliance: https://www.scrumalliance.org/community/articles/ 2011/september/applying-to-become-a-csc

Block, P. (1993). *Stewardship: Choosing Service Over Self Interest.*

Bressen, T. (2005-2007). *Group Facilitation Premier.* Eugene, OR: www.treegroup.info.

Cohn, M. (2005). *Agile Estimating and Planning.* Prentice Hall PTR.

Cohn, M. (2012). *A Weighty Matter for the Daily Scrum.* Retrieved from Mountain Goat Software: http://www.mountaingoatsoftware.com/blog/weight y-matter-daily-scrum

Cohn, M. (n.d.). *Sprint Planning Meeting.* Retrieved from Mountain Goat Software: https://www.mountaingoatsoftware.com/agile/scrum /sprint-planning-meeting

DeMarco, T. (1987). *Peopleware: Productive Projects and Teams.* Addison-Wesley Professional.

Deza, M., & Deza, E. (2009). *Encyclopedia of Distances.*

Doran, G. (1981). There's a S.M.A.R.T. way to write management's goals and objectives. *Management Review, 70*(11), 35–36.

Dreyfus, H., & Dreyfus, S. (1986). *Mind over machine: The power of human intuition and expertise in the era of the computer.* Free Press.

Greenleaf, R. (1991). *The Servant as Leader.*

Hiromoto, H. (n.d.). Retrieved from Scrum Orgánico: http://www.scrumorganico.com

Hohmann, L. (2006). *Innovation Games: Creating Breakthrough Products Through Collaborative Play.* Addison-Wesley Professional.

Kaner, S. (2007). *Facilitator's Guide to Participatory Decision-Making* (2nd Edition ed.). Jossey-Bass.

Kerth, N. L. (2001). *Project Retrospectives: A Handbook for Team Reviews.* Dorset House.

King, B. (1998). *The Idea Edge.*

Kofman, F. (2013). *Conscious Business.* Sounds True.

Laloux, F. (2014). *Reinventing Organizations.* Nelson Parker.

Larsen, D., & Derby, E. (2006). *Agile Retrospectives: Making Good Teams Great.*

McKergow, M. (2014). *Host.* Solutions Books.

Moore, G. (2006). *Crossing the Chasm.* HarperBusiness.

Nielsen, L. (n.d.). *Personas.* Retrieved from Interaction Design Foundation: https://www.interaction-design.org/literature/book/the-encyclopedia-of-human-computer-interaction-2nd-ed/personas

Olalla, J. (2000). *Lingüística de Emociones y Estados de Ánimo.* The Newfield Network.

Owen, H. (2008). *Open Space Technology: A User's Guide.*

Patton, J. (2008). *The new user story backlog is a map.* Retrieved from Agile Product Design: http://www.agileproductdesign.com/blog/the_new_backlog.html

Patton, J., & Economy, P. (2014). *User Story Mapping: Discover the Whole Story, Build the Right Product.* O'Reilly Media.

Pichler, R. (2010). *Agile Product Management with Scrum.* Addison-Wesley Professional.

PMI. (2013). *PMBOK® guide.* (5, Ed.) Project Management Institute.

Rasmusson, J. (2010). *The Agile Samurai.* Pragmatic Bookshelf.

Schein, E. (2010). *Organizational Culture and Leadership.* Jossey-Bass.

Schwaber, K., & Beedle , M. (2001). *Agile Software Development with Scrum.* Pearson.

Schwaber, K., & Sutherland, J. (2013, July). *Scrum Guide.* Retrieved from Scrum Guides: http://www.scrumguides.org/

Schwarz, R. (2002). *The Skilled Facilitator.* Jossey-Bass.

Senge, P. (2012). *La Quinta Disciplina.* Granica.

Spears, L. (2000). On Character and Servant-Leadership: Ten Characteristics of Effective, Caring Leaders. *Concepts & Connections, 8*(3).

Sutherland, J. (2014). *Definition of Done.* Retrieved from Scrum Inc.: https://www.scruminc.com/definition-of-done/

Sutherland, J. (2014). *Definition Of Ready.* Retrieved from Scrum Inc.: http://www.scruminc.com/definition-of-ready/

Ulwick, A. (2005). *What Customers Want.* McGraw-Hill Education.

Wake, B. (2003, Agosto 17). *INVEST in good stories and SMART tasks.* Retrieved from XP123: Exploring Extreme Programming: http://xp123.com/articles/invest-in-good-stories-and-smart-tasks/

www.ingramcontent.com/pod-product-compliance
Lightning Source LLC
Chambersburg PA
CBHW061157240326
R18026500001B/R180265PG41519CBX00025B/43